Judges Under Fire

Judges Under Fire

Human Rights, Independent Judges, and the **Rule of Law**

HAROLD BAER, JR.

AMERICAN BAR ASSOCIATION
Section of
Dispute Resolution

14 13 12 11 10 5 4 3 2 1

Library of Congress Cataloguing-in-Publication Data is on file with the Library of Congress.

ISBN 978-1-61632-803-0

Discounts are available for books ordered in bulk. Special consideration is given to state bars, CLE programs, and other bar-related organizations. Inquire at Book Publishing, ABA Publishing, American Bar Association, 321 North Clark Street, Chicago, Illinois 60654.

www.ababooks.org

For

Suzanne Baer

who, for better than a half century,

has personified the old Chinese proverb:

A man's best possession is a sympathetic wife.

CONTENTS

PREFACE

THIS SLIM VOLUME SEEKS TO ILLUSTRATE WHAT CAN HAPPEN WHEN the judiciary is stripped of its independence and prevented from following the rule of law. While it provides some lessons from foreign nations where the rule of law has been sublimated to opportunistic leaders who are ambitious and self-dealing, it also provides a chilling reminder that it can happen here.

The vitality of the rule of law was a major concern of Chief Justice John G. Roberts, Jr., in his 2007 Year-End Report on the Federal Judiciary, in which he wrote:

> Most Americans are far too busy to spend much time pondering the role of the United States Judiciary—they simply and understandably expect the court system to work. But as we begin the New Year, I ask a moment's reflection on how our country might look in the absence of a skilled and independent Judiciary. We do not need to look far beyond our borders, or beyond the front page of any newspaper, to see what is at stake.
>
> More than two hundred years after the American Revolution, much of the world remains subject to judicial systems that provide doubtful opportunities for challenging government action as contrary to law, or receiving a fair adjudication

of criminal charges, or securing a fair remedy for wrongful injury, or protecting rights in property, or obtaining an impartial resolution of a commercial dispute. Many foreign judges cannot exercise independent judgment on matters of law without fear of reprisal or removal.

Americans should take enormous pride in our judicial system. But there is no cause for complacency. Our judicial system inspires the world because of the commitment of each new generation of judges who build upon the vision and accomplishments of those who came before.

Judges must embrace their roles as the primary advocates in the pursuit of judicial independence. To a large extent, they control their own fates and the fate of the rule of law. Judges cannot be expected, however, to carry that burden alone. Indeed, while these pages portray heroic acts by individual judges, the message underlying these stories is the need for constant vigilance by the public—vigilance to ensure that we never fall prey to the kind of unscrupulous leadership that has caused so much damage to the rule of law around the world.

No matter how well designed or well intentioned a government appears to be, its survival is always in the hands of the public. These stories accentuate that concept and add the ingredient of fragility. We must continually remember how easy it is for a country, including our own, to lose its way.

One cannot create democracy with a piece of paper or guarantee freedom simply by adopting a written constitution. Human rights cannot be protected solely by declarations. It takes committed and courageous people and independent and courageous judges to ensure the survival not only of human rights but of all our fundamental liberties.

Looking around the world today, I realize how many countries that claim to have embraced the rule of law are yet to guaranty an independent judiciary. Purporting to have established systems of justice that are constitutional, they leave human rights constantly at risk, and justice often appears to be of secondary importance. This realization is what made me decide to write this book—to try to persuade thinking citizens and leaders alike that justice, liberty, and freedom depend in large measure on an independent, effective judiciary. This book presents examples to show that this is not a pious platitude but a fundamental requirement.

Clearly, as you will soon see, it is not my intent to demonstrate that the United States has a flawless system of judicial independence that all other countries should follow, for while we have the proper framework to ensure judicial independence, any system—and there are many countries with well-designed systems—can and does fail where there is a lack of careful and continual nurturing and respect. Indeed, my intention is to share, through one of this book's chapters, an experience I had only a few years ago that made me realize just how precious and delicate our system is and how crucial it is to remain true to that system—especially when it is tested, pressured, or even threatened.

The case of *United States v. Bayless* demonstrated to me, first-hand, that even a solid system such as ours, which includes proper protections and fosters judicial independence, can be jeopardized. This, my own judicial apocalypse, occurred when extremely power-ful forces—including the president of the United States—joined to publicly attack and pressure me to abandon my independence as a judge. The onslaught began simply because I refused to com-promise my beliefs. Here, my goal was to prevent police abuse of human rights.

The ordeal made me realize that even our system—the system we believe to be the envy of the world—may not be as stable as we would like to think. In response, I looked around the world for other examples where the rule of law is imperiled and an independent judiciary is only a dream.

To set the stage, I interviewed a Chinese lawyer—a lawyer who had fled his homeland because he could no longer adhere to the rule of law and was tormented for trying. While that might seem out of context, it really is not. The plight of lawyers who strive to uphold the profession's passion for justice is the same all over the world. When a totalitarian government imposes its will on the judiciary, there is no room for the good lawyer to practice and to practice independently and without interference. In short, courageous members of the bar deserve a place of honor in this book.

All that being said, I share former Supreme Court Justice Sandra Day O'Connor's dream that she wrote of in her 2003 memoir, *The Majesty of the Law:*

> I am optimistic about the world our children will discover. At a time of heightened interest in a new global order, various countries around the world have made enormous strides in the effort to build a fair and equitable social order that affords all children and adults political freedom, economic opportunity, and meaningful legal protection.

As I have pondered how we can achieve those goals, I have come face to face with the hard reality that no democracy, no constitution, and no rule of law can build an equitable social order without courageous judges and an independent bar. While the United States has positioned itself as a global archetype of such a system, it is far from perfect, and many other countries have a long, long way to go.

As we start, then, let us keep in mind the words of one of our wisest federal jurists, Judge Learned Hand:

I often wonder whether we do not rest our hopes too much upon constitutions, upon laws and upon courts. These are false hopes; believe me, these are false hopes. Liberty lies in the hearts of men and women; when it dies there, no constitution, no law, no court can save it; no constitution, no law, no court can even do much to help it. While it lies there it needs no constitution, no law, no court to save it.

INTRODUCTION

"He has made Judges dependent on his Will alone, for the tenure of their offices, and the amount and payment of their salaries."

IN THOSE FEW WORDS IN THE DECLARATION OF INDEPENDENCE, Thomas Jefferson proclaimed America's call for judicial independence. Condemning tyrannical control and abuse of justice, Jefferson's words anticipated the constitutional reform on which our system of justice is based—guaranteed tenure and compensation. In this book, Harold Baer, Jr., makes the case for extending judicial independence around the world. Without it, democratic governments and the rule of law cannot succeed.

This is a book about freedom, justice, and compassion. The author is amply endowed with these qualities, and he is just the right person to write this book.

United States District Judge Harold Baer, Jr., was born and raised in a household that personified and practiced belief in these three values. Both of his parents lived by them—both were active in the 1940s and '50s in social-welfare work and minority-party politics in New York City. His father became a widely respected New York State Supreme Court justice. Harold Jr. came by his integrity and commitment to fairness naturally, and they have guided him throughout his years of public service as a federal prosecutor, New York state court judge, and federal judge.

Some years ago, before he became a judge, Harold and I jointly taught an adult-education course on criminal justice at the New School for Social Research in New York City. There were about twenty students in the class, which met for two hours once a week. One evening, we focused on the topic of criminal sentencing, and we invited a guest to attend our class. The guest arrived early and we put him in a seat in the back of the room. Harold then described to the students a state criminal prosecution for illegal possession of a handgun.

The defendant in the case was a nineteen-year-old man who grew up in a low-income area in the Bedford-Stuyvesant section of Brooklyn. After he dropped out of high school, he served briefly in the U.S. Navy, but he was dishonorably discharged for going absent without leave (AWOL). His reading level was limited to comic books.

One summer evening, the defendant was present when a fight broke out among a group of young people gathered around a brownstone stoop in his neighborhood. A shot was fired and one of the young men fell dead. The defendant denied any involvement in the shooting, but he admitted that the pistol that fired the fatal shot belonged to him. It had been a warm evening and his jacket had been hanging on the stoop railing, with the pistol in the outside pocket. The young man surrendered to the police and was charged with homicide.

Eventually the defendant was persuaded by his assigned Legal Aid lawyer to plead guilty to illegal gun possession. The lawyer had explained to him the risks of going to trial on the homicide charge and the possibility of conviction and a sentence of life in prison.

At this point in his description of the crime and defense, Harold asked members of the class what sentence each would impose on the defendant if they were the judge. Most of the class members recommended long prison terms, pronouncing the defendant incorrigible because of his AWOL history.

A few said they needed more information about the defendant before making a decision on the appropriate sentence.

Harold then invited our guest to come forward and introduced him to the class as the actual defendant in the case. The guest described how he had pleaded guilty to the gun charge and was sentenced to five to ten years in the state prison in Auburn, New York.

He told the class that he promised himself he would never go to jail again. Through the prison library, he successfully completed high school and college equivalency courses; he became the scribe for illiterate prisoners who wanted to write home, and then he traded the cigarettes he received in exchange to purchase a Dale Carnegie success book, which he read several times from cover to cover. He was eventually paroled and went to work as a dental assistant on Staten Island. He applied for and landed a job with the Vera Institute of Justice and helped administer its work-release program. Eventually he was promoted to director of Vera's Manhattan work-release program, with a budget of more than a million dollars.

The class members broke into applause.

The class session demonstrated the importance of treating each case and each individual with understanding and judicial restraint in balancing the interests of the particular individual and the interests of the community, rather than simply imposing severe draconian punishment.

It was a perfect case study of how fairness and compassion in the criminal justice system can produce positive results. (Our guest was later hired by the Federal Bureau of Prisons to work at a facility in Colorado, and after that he became the Director of Prisons in one of the heavily populated states.)

Judge Baer has demonstrated his own commitment to fairness and compassion in many ways. When he was Chief of the Criminal Division in the United States Attorney's office in the Southern District of New York, he instituted the first federal work-release program. He served as the first executive director of the New York City Police Department's Civilian Complaint Review Board (reviewing complaints of police officers). To give minority law students a chance to work inside the judicial system, he and his wife, Suzanne, initiated—in concert with the New York County Bar Association—the first judicial intern program specifically for them. He has successfully advocated state legislation that will allow those men and women convicted in federal court to more quickly regain the right to licensed employment. Early in 2010, he helped begin and then headed the first re-entry program in the Southern District of New York to help ex-offenders get started and avoid recidivating after their release from custody.

There are few people who can speak with more authority on the need for establishing and defending judicial independence in order to create a free democratic society and make any system of justice work as it should.

Whitney North Seymour, Jr
New York
July 2010

1

How Patrick Sellar
Cleared the Highlands

This story is about the evictions of the residents from Strath-naver, in Scotland, and about the trial of Patrick Sellar—a man hired by the Countess of Sutherland to clear the land of settlers. It is a story about undue influence in the justice system, and how the law failed to recognize the plight of the powerless.

World history has seen countless populations removed from homes and villages. The term "removal" is a hopelessly inadequate euphemism for what often constitutes bloody eradication or genocide. In some cases, these events occur when people find ways to circumvent the law or even reject it outright. In other cases, however, the legal system is implicated in the slaughter. In the case of the Scottish Highland Clearances, in which thousands of families—without compensation and against their will—were removed to coastal villages, the legal system effected and condoned the displacement.

IN THE EIGHTEENTH CENTURY, SCOTLAND WAS A BEAUTIFUL, PASTO-ral nation of hardworking people—as it is today. On the country's northern Highlands, near the Strathnaver valley, farmers worked the land between majestic, misty mountains. Today, historical markers speckle the drive amid acres of open pasture from Loch Naver to Farr Bay.

A Stalwart People Are Driven from Their Homes

This lush valley was once home to the Scottish McKays and other clans, numbering in the thousands, some of whom could trace their ancestors as far back as early medieval times. For centuries, these Scots had farmed under the rule of chiefs and then landlords, fought for the Scottish and British crowns, and persevered despite the ruthless winters and famines of the Highlands. They developed an identity closely linked to the land they worked, for they drew sustenance from it.

Today, these stalwart people have all but vanished from the Highlands. Evicted two centuries ago from their parents' hard-fought inheritance, they braved new lives in North America and Australia and are sprinkled around the globe. While their ancestral homes are gone, their legacy remains etched on tombstones of Grumberg, surrounded by grazing sheep.

In the late eighteenth century, the Scottish Highlands were still home to feudal societies. The king and aristocracy—"lairds"—owned title to the land. Large parcels were allocated to factors, who managed the land and paid rents to the aristocracy. In turn, the factors further subdivided the land, renting it to tenants and subtenants, who farmed it. Even during times of relative plenty, pulling sustenance from the land was a hardscrabble existence. And when the land and the skies refused to cooperate with the toiling farmers, life became truly onerous.

Peasant families lived and worked on small plots for decades without ever gaining title to the land or any rights to the fruits of their labor. Most occupied the land only as "tenants-at-will." This meant that upon minimal notice they could be expelled at the will of the landowners. A few had arranged primitive lease agreements—called "tack" agreements—with landowners, but the landowners could easily intimidate tenants into repudiating the agreements, or they could simply wait for the year terms to expire and then fail to renew them.

Ancient and ill-considered, the extraordinarily foolish system was wasteful in economic terms, not to mention costly on generations of Scots, who had little to show for centuries of toil. It also left enormous numbers of farmers completely vulnerable during periods of poor harvest. Farmers could not make plans for the future; they were captive to the whims—whether wise or foolish—of the landowners.

Agrarian reforms were beginning in England and Lowland Scotland. Small farms were merging into larger cooperatives, and new modes of production were being implemented. In many entire regions, such reforms replaced crops with cattle, sheep, or other livestock. This necessitated clearing farmland to create pastures for grazing. The reforms were, in part, based on Scottish Enlightenment ideas that were beginning to change the way Scotland and the western world viewed markets and economics. Lairds who had formerly considered themselves "guardians" of the land and its occupants began to see themselves as merely landowners. Responsibility for farming, which had long been reciprocal between laird and tenant, became unidirectional: The land had value, but the peasants were obstructing the mining of such value.

As the eighteenth century turned into the nineteenth, the Countess of Sutherland, Laird of the Highlands, realized that the Highlands' agrarian society, which was still largely uninfluenced by the agricultural revolution occurring in other parts of Scotland, could benefit from such reforms. The Highlands had recently suffered a string of harsh winters and widespread famine, which had not only hit peasants hard in the stomach but had hit the gentry in the pocketbook. As the land produced less, the peasants had less to eat and the gentry had less income. Predictably, the gentry worried more about their dwindling pocketbooks and less about the peasants' well-being.

At the same time, in the United Kingdom and Europe, the demand for wool had been growing. The countess saw this as an opportunity to increase her net worth. Accordingly, she decided that the Highlands should move away from the cultivation of crops and cattle and toward the production of wool. In her defense, she also believed that profits from wool production could not only grow her wealth but could help the remote Highlands develop and compete with the rapidly changing Lowlands region. Indeed, the views propounded by famous Scottish economist and moralist Adam Smith, which influenced the economic reforms, would prove to be valuable in the long run, even if disastrous in the short term. As it turned out, the evil was not in the ideas behind the reform, but in its execution.

Communities Cleared of Fifteen Thousand

The countess invited entrepreneurs from around Scotland to determine what types of reforms were needed and how they could be implemented. Patrick Sellar was among those who traveled north to the Highlands to offer proposals. Like the countess, he and others believed that the Highlands could be extremely profitable if the fragmented parcels of land could be joined across the inland terrain to create larger parcels for sheep pastures. However, this would require not only clearing existing communities but entirely eradicating small-plot farming.

The countess appointed the entrepreneurs to leadership positions in the inland and coastal regions. It was agreed that the inland factors would be responsible for removing the communities and demolishing any infrastructure that would impede grazing or migration of livestock. To absorb the thousands of peasant families displaced from their plots, those on the coast would create new communities. Naively, the gentry assumed that, despite never having lived by the water or engaged in deep-sea fishing, the unsettled farmers would simply take up fishing or some other new profession.

In reality, life on the North Sea was unpredictable, terrifying, and distinctly hazardous. In a series of letters entitled "Gloomy Memories" in the Edinburgh *Weekly Chronicle*, Donald MacLeod described the environmental and living conditions waiting for new settlers on the coastal region:

> People accustomed to witness only the quiet friths and petty heavings of the sea, from lowland shores, can form little conception of the gigantic workings of the Northern sea, which, from a comparatively placid state, often rises suddenly without apparent cause, into mountainous billows; and, when north winds prevail, its appearance becomes terrific beyond description. To this raging element, however, the poor people were now compelled to look for their subsistence, or starve, which was the only other alternative.

Moreover, in addition to their lack of practical experience in drawing sustenance from the sea, the new settlers were astoundingly ill-equipped. MacLeod noted that "not a shilling" of the £210,000 supposedly allotted to improving the Highlanders' new homeland went toward buying boats or other fishing equipment to improve their quality of life. Rather, the money was spent on "roads, bridges, inns, and manses . . . for the accommodation of the new gentlemen tenantry and clergy." Macleod ruefully concludes that "[n]othing . . . could seem more helpless, than the attempt to draw subsistence from such a boisterous sea with such means as they possessed, and in the most complete ignorance of sea-faring matters." It was truly a hostile and unwelcoming new home.

Technically Correct but Inhumane

By 1814, Patrick Sellar had become an inland factor. He was charged with preparing the removal of Strathnaver's existing communities, and he proceeded to expel tenants-at-will. Then, upon the expiration of any existing tacks, he revoked those agreements, enabling him to repossess the land and prepare it for sheep-farming. While people were to be compensated for their homes, Sellar did not consider it necessary to conduct further negotiations with the tenants, because the countess was legally entitled to repossess the land at lease-end. Sellar's strict legal conception of the situation may have been technically correct, but his failure to consider the human toll of his actions would prove to be a critical mistake.

The damage caused by the proposed plan was compounded by a failure to give sufficient notice before the removals were to begin. As the common-folk spoke primarily Gaelic, the English-speaking aristocracy relied on the region's clergy to convey the message announcing the impending removals, and also to conduct all negotiations about terms of the removals. The preceding winter had been especially harsh, and the clergy had been successful through the spring in postponing the removals. But Sellar, eager to please his laird and wary of missing the gravy train, grew anxious and refused to extend the deadline any further.

Interestingly, the countess was not particularly fond of Sellar. In fact, she had remarked in letters to her husband that she found Sellar to be harsh and potentially unqualified for his assigned task. But when the peasant farmers appealed to her personally because Sellar had refused to bargain further, she refused—even though she had already overridden one refusal by Sellar to push back the date. The removals would begin, with Sellar at the helm.

Homes Are Set Aflame

On Sunday of the second week of June in 1814, the parishioners of Langdale church gathered on a lush green slope alongside the rushing River Naver. The early morning sun broke over Strathnaver mountain, softly lighting the paths between the rolling hills that would lead the disconsolate congregants from their cherished homes to the strange new land by the sea. The beauty of the summer day made the anticipated farewell all the more bitter. In his journal, the Reverend Donald Sage, who presided over Sunday services at the church at Achness, recorded his deep sense of impending loss:

> The service began. The very aspect of the congregation was itself a sermon, and a most impressive one. Old Achoul sat right opposite to me. As my eye fell upon his venerable countenance, bearing the impress of eighty-seven winters, I was deeply affected, and could scarcely articulate the Psalm.
>
> I preached and the people listened, but every sentence uttered and heard was in opposition to the tide of our natural feelings, which, setting in against us, mounted at every step of our progress higher and higher. At last, all restraints were compelled to give way. The preacher ceased to speak, the people to listen.
>
> All lifted up their voices and wept, mingling their tears together. It was indeed the place of parting, and the hour. The greater number parted never again to behold each other in the land of the living.

Sage was, unfortunately, prescient in his prediction. Seller departed from his plan for a relatively orderly exodus. Instead, he chose to flex the substantial muscle of his position of authority. Only a month after the factors had begun notifying the Highlanders of the removals, "the work of devastation" (to use MacLeod's terms) was under way. Lawmen rode horses from town to town—Farr, Rogart, Golspie, and Kildonan—setting fire to house after house, until nearly three hundred homes were aflame. Smoke and fire choked panicked inhabitants, creating, in MacLeod's description, a scene unlike any he had ever seen:

> The cries of the women and children—the roaring of the affrighted cattle, hunted at the same time by the yelling dogs of the shepherds amid the smoke and fire—altogether presented a scene that completely baffles description: it requires to be seen to be believed . . . It would be an endless task to give a detail of the sufferings of families or individuals during this calamitous period; or to describe its dreadful consequences on the health and lives of the victims.

Many villagers had been stricken with a typhus fever that had swept the countryside, which made removing them from the burning homes, not to mention transporting them afterward, truly onerous. By day's end, hundreds of families were homeless. On the peaceful moor that had raised generations of Scots, precious few homes remained.

By the following Tuesday, only about two dozen families lucky enough to miss the initial wave of removals were still living in the village of Strathnaver. Of these, most had sick or elderly relatives, or young children who could not be moved. In one household, a pregnant woman, late in term and undergoing complications, was immobile and helpless. In another, ninety-year-old Margaret McKay's family could not coax her out of her home, for she had lived her entire life in the village and expected to die there. As it turned out, the poor old woman got her wish, albeit sooner than she would have liked, and undoubtedly not in the fashion she would have preferred.

On Wednesday, shrouded in inky pre-dawn darkness, sheriff's men, carrying axes and blazing torches and under orders from Sellar, entered the village on horseback and rode to each of the remaining homes. They clipped the wooden pins of the thatched roofs so they collapsed on whatever and whomever was within, at which point the lawmen ignited them. They proceeded through the village until every house was swallowed in flames and thick black smoke.

In those early hours, a young boy watched the grisly scene from a nearby hill. He later described to a London newspaper how roofs collapsed over the heads of sleeping men, women, and children, and how the roaring flames could not drown out the screams for mercy from within. He reported how a family pulled an old woman from smoldering heaps of mud and thatch, only to watch her take her last breath, and how he saw a young pregnant woman, writhing in pain on the blackened ground, miscarry her infant.

". . . Never Saw the Like Done Before . . ."

Word of the brutal Strathnaver removals spread across the Highlands and beyond. Until this time, since commoners had no legal standing to challenge the evictions, displacement of inland farming communities had met with little resistance. Strathnaver became a watershed event, however, fostering widespread opposition to the entire Scottish Land Improvement Plan. In faraway London, newspapers provided rapt audiences with details of the ruthless campaign, instantaneously igniting a public outcry.

In the wake of the wave of public sentiment, a local prosecutor who had butted heads with Sellar on previous occasions brought charges against him for destruction of property and negligent homicide. The legal action troubled the countess, who worried that the entire improvement plan might be in jeopardy, not to mention the possibility that she might be implicated in the fiasco. Accordingly, despite Sellar's pleas for assistance, she distanced herself from him, declaring that if he was guilty of the crimes charged he ought to be brought to justice. Other factors, however, fearing that their actions might be scrutinized, became actively interested in seeing Sellar acquitted.

Preparations for the trial lasted almost two years, during which the prosecutor gathered witness testimony from thirty-five local peasants and clergy members. The story that began to unfold was quite remarkable in its savagery. For months before the tragic day of the removals, Sellar had been burning farmland, running cattle off pasture lands, and tormenting residents. Witnesses described how Sellar's men turned women and children out of their homes during the day, while the men were in the fields, without providing them temporary shelter. One seventy-six-year-old woman claimed that she had paid rents to the factors for more than sixty years. On the day of the removals, she explained, she crawled from the ruins of her burning home only to see Seller's hatchet-men destroying the food stocks and crops that she had saved for subsistence in her old age. Several bystanders, aware of Sellar's severe treatment, alleged that he ignored pleas for mercy on behalf of the sick and elderly by responding "with fury and rage . . . giv[ing] orders that [a sick woman] might instantly be turned out whatever the consequences might be, or that he would order the house pulled down around her ears."

The prosecutor also interviewed the sheriff's deputies employed to carry out the clearances. They admitted that they knew well enough that what they were doing was wrong, that they ". . . never saw the like done before . . ." and that they had complied solely out of dread of Sellar's authority. They also confirmed that Sellar had not only authorized the brutal clearances, but was physically present as the houses burned. A deputy explained that he carried out Sellar's orders despite his moral concerns, because "all was right under such a man of law," and Sellar's position as a factor gave him innate credibility.

With the full weight of public opinion against him, Sellar grew increasingly worried about his chances in court. He repeatedly attempted to settle the case, but the peasant-plaintiffs were dead set on being heard in open court. This was a rare, perhaps unprecedented, opportunity for commoners to seek legal redress against an aristocrat.

The date of the trial was set for April 23, 1816. Sellar, trying to rehabilitate his reputation before the trial, wrote long letters to fellow factors and to the press, arguing that the charges were exaggerated and that he had compensated the owners of damaged homes. He also denied that he dealt inhumanely with the people of Strathnaver, claiming that he was actually sparing them the inhumanity of dealing with the winters, famine, and drought of their ancestral territory. As the trial began, he could only hope that his public relations efforts had influenced someone.

Early on April 23, Sellar was led from Dornoch jail to the courtroom at Inverness, where he and his defense team took their places before the bench. Rain pelted the long glass windows, diffusing the gray light of the overcast sky and casting blurred shadows on the gallery of witnesses inside. London and Edinburgh newspaper reporters wedged into wooden benches, poised to transcribe the most anticipated trial in Great Britain. This was not only the trial of Patrick Sellar, but of the entire Scottish Land Improvement Plan. Other peasants who had been ejected from their farms and forced to cobble together new lives in strange new lands looked to the judge, hoping for some sort of validation of their worth or rights.

By 10:00 a.m., the courtroom's capacity was exceeded. Bits of Gaelic and English mingled in excited chatter as the crown's prosecutor ushered in a hesitant husband and wife. The prosecutor made some attempt at reassurances, but the family, speaking only a local dialect of Gaelic, made no sign of recognition. A clergyman, acting as translator, gently guided the anxious couple to a secluded corner near the jury box.

A moment later, the bailiff's clear voice rose above the gallery's persistent murmur to announce the entrance of the presiding judge, Lord Pitmilly. Ruddy and round, the judge effused affluence and entitlement—a striking contrast with the humble and demure commoners. As the courtroom fell silent, the judge sternly surveyed the faces of gentry, journalists, and peasants and immediately called for assembly of the jury—fifteen "gentlemen drawn from outwith Sutherland." Representatives of Scottish landholders whose own fortunes were, unfortunately, integrally linked to the outcome of the trial, they took their places in the jury box. Without delay, the judge lambasted the newspapers for their coverage of the case against Sellar and their sympathetic treatment of the peasant farmers. As his condemnation rambled on, it became clear that the interests of the aristocracy had taken root, and that the trial would likely be marred by such outside interests.

Standing uncertainly in the defendant's box, Sellar heard the bailiff read the charges against him. The litany of crimes included property damage and the negligent homicides of Donald McBeath and Margaret McKay. At the time of the removals, both had been elderly residents, confined to bed, whom families and neighbors had been unable to pull from the flames. Margaret's daughter and son-in-law, Mr. and Mrs. Chisholm, sat beside the jury, ready to lend their accounts of her terrifying last minutes of life.

Murder Charges Dropped

Questioned separately through the clergyman interpreter, both Chisholms vividly described the destruction and mayhem of that June morning two years earlier—how they tried to save their mother but failed to reach her before the dense smoke choked away her life. Eleven other witnesses also testified to the brutal force used to evict the Strathnaver people. However, their testimony occasionally conflicted, possibly due to problems with translation, and several corroborating witnesses were not present. In the end, the prosecution could not marshal enough evidence to support the charges— that Sellar was the direct cause of the deaths—and was forced to drop the murder charges. If Sellar was to be held accountable at all for his brutality, only the property charges remained.

Sellar's defense attorneys brought forward five character witnesses: two proprietors, two lawmen, and a merchant. Each vouched for Sellar's "character for humanity." In addition, even though the crown had already dropped the murder charges, Sellar introduced witnesses to ridicule the peasants' testimony. Interestingly, the defendant's case, while designed to show that Sellar could not have committed murder, conceded most of the points made in the crown's characterization of events. Apparently the only point on which the prosecution and defense disagreed was whether Sellar was legally entitled to forcibly remove the tenant-farmers. The defendant's unconventional strategy showed a startling degree of confidence. It was the first hint that outsiders with interests in the outcome of the case might have unduly influenced the proceedings.

The extent of the bias became evident when, in a shocking departure from the norm, Lord Pitmilly himself assumed responsibility for summing up the evidence for the jury. He told them that the law allowed Sellar to burn down barns and eject tenants. He reminded them that Mr. and Mrs. Chisholm's testimony had been contradictory and instructed them to treat such evidence with skepticism. Finally, he noted that if jury members were unsure about the facts of the case, they must look to the defendant's character, "for this is always important in balancing contradictory behavior." He remarked that the real evidence was that Patrick Sellar was the kind of man who cared for the sick and elderly. In the minds of the jury, his commentary left no doubt as to which side the court had taken. Within fifteen minutes of retiring to the jury room, the jury returned a verdict: innocent on all counts.

Lord Pitmilly warmly concurred. He addressed Mr. Sellar with an apology of sorts:

> Mr. Sellar, it is now my duty to dismiss you from the bar; and you have the satisfaction of thinking, that you are discharged by the unanimous opinion of the Jury and the Court. I am sure that, although your feelings must have been agitated, you cannot regret that this took place; and I am hopeful it will have due effect on the minds of the country, which have been so much and so improperly agitated.

After two years of public posturing, tension, and evidence-gathering, the trial was over in less than fifteen hours. Patrick Sellar was a free man. Never again would he wield the almost limitless power that had allowed him, godlike, to hold the lives of others in his hands. He lived out his years on his Sutherland estate, earning a healthy income from sheep-farming in the reinvented economy of the region.

Two Pillars of Justice Compromised

The story of the Highland Clearances is a story of the rule of law gone awry. Here was a policy with obvious benefits for aristocrats and potential, albeit less clear, benefits for peasants. Under the improvement plan, the countess should have gained a new-and-improved, more profitable tract of land. The peasant farmers should have found new, more lucrative professions in the revitalized economy of the region and experienced an improved quality of life. Instead, the avarice of a small number of powerful individuals, and the failure of others in power to keep them in line, compromised the potential benefits of the plan and transformed it into a weapon. When Sellar wielded that weapon unchecked, the result was thousands of miserable, displaced families, burned homes, and lives brutally cut short. As the philosopher Edmund Burke, who was writing in Sellar's own lifetime, famously remarked: "The only thing necessary for the triumph of evil is for good men to do nothing."

This raises two questions: With feudal tenants almost entirely lacking substantive property rights, could a courageous judge actually have made any difference? Could he have saved any lives? The short answer to these questions is yes: If a courageous judge had intervened, he could have prevented many of the hardships suffered by the peasants. True, in the short term his influence might have been limited. Without an expansion of underlying substantive property laws that would allow commoners to hold title in land, the judge could not prevent removal from the land, but he might have been able to ensure it was done in a humane and sensible manner.

Furthermore, and most obviously, a courageous and independent judge would not have capitulated to the special interests—the factors and landowners—and would have held Sellar and his superiors responsible for the horrible consequences of their actions.

Such a decision by the judge would never have brought back Margaret McKay or any of the others who lost their lives, but it would, at the very least, have provided a tacit acknowledgment that their lives had meaning. As it turned out, they did not even receive that ultimate dignity.

Finally, had a courageous judge presided over Sellar's trial and decided the case based on the rule of law and the facts and evidence before him, rather than yielding to outside influences, the decision might have acted as a catalyst for the eventual expansion of tenants' rights. Scotland did not begin to dismantle the feudal system, however, until legislation in 1974 effectively prevented new feudalities. Then, after England's Scotland Act of 1998 established Scotland's own Parliament in 1999, one of the new government's first objectives was to rid Scotland of the archaic system of land ownership. Its comprehensive Abolition of Feudal Tenure Act of 2000 ended centuries of feudalism once and for all.

One has to wonder whether the regime would have crumbled earlier if a courageous judge, rather than Lord Pitmilly, had presided at Sellar's trial. With the eyes of all of Great Britain on his courtroom, Pitmilly had a rare opportunity to let everyone know the real cause of the horror at Strathnaver—the feudal system that fettered the workers of the land and kept them mired in poverty and subservient to the greed of the ruling elite and the ambition of a ruthless social climber. But Pitmilly stayed silent. Worse, in fact, he blamed the victims.

In the end, the Sellar trial showed how two pillars of justice were compromised. Pillar one—the presumptively objective jury—turned out to be hopelessly representative of only the ruling class. Pillar two—the judge, supposed to be unbiased and objective at all times—showed active prejudice from the opening statements to the closing arguments and at every moment in between. The prosecutor wrote afterward that the trial had been "a conflict between the law and the resistance to the law," because it pitted the legal rights of the landholders against the rights (or lack of rights) of the tenants. In Scotland's collective consciousness, however, the trial represents a moment in history when the law ignored the plight of the powerless in favor of preserving the prerogative of the powerful. It would not be the last time.

2

Judicial Independence in the American Colonies

Writing in his Almanac of Liberty more than two hundred years after the events described in this chapter, Justice William O. Douglas said, "The episode [with William Cosby] was one of the grievances listed in the Declaration of Independence: 'He has made Judges dependent on his Will alone, for the tenure of their offices.'"

What Lewis Morris said and did about the miscreant Governor Cosby had a lasting influence. It helped make firm the American maxim that courts cannot be made a tool of executive power and that they can be established only by a legislature that represents the popular will.

LEWIS MORRIS WAS TIRED OF WAITING TO PRESENT HIS CASE TO THE Privy Council of King George II. Confident that his mission would be a success, he had sailed from New Jersey to England late in 1734, traveling with a carefully assembled indictment of his chief political rival, William Cosby, the royal governor of New York. Now it was almost November of 1735.

Morris's mission was twofold. He was in London first and foremost to represent New Yorkers who held grievances against Cosby and, if all went well, to have him recalled as governor. On a far more personal level, however, Morris sought to be reinstated as chief justice of New York's supreme court, a position from which Cosby had removed him two years earlier.

Morris had painstakingly prepared his plea to the king's advisers. In his mind, he must have seen Cosby's corrupt tenure in New York coming to an end. He most likely thought personal vindication was also imminent. But for now, the sixty-four-year-old judge and veteran of New York's political scene could do nothing but wait for his voice to be heard. And now that a year of delays had kept his case from the Privy Council, the enthusiasm with which Morris had set sail from New Jersey was giving way to frustration.

Morris revealed his impatience in a letter to his friend and political ally James Alexander, who had also opposed Governor Cosby and had served as attorney general of both the New York and New Jersey colonies: "Applications here by the delays it will . . . meet with and the expences attending of it will be so great as to render the remedy worse than the disease: So that a man had almost better sit down with the losse of a great part of what he has, than Spend the remainder in an Endeavour for relief wch. (if at all to be had) will be So long in coming that as to render it almost ineffectual."

The Case Against Governor Cosby

Despite the frustration caused by the seemingly interminable delay, Morris had reason for hope. The case against Royal Governor William Cosby was strong, and everyone knew it. Writing again to Alexander, Morris noted the ill regard in which even Cosby's allies in London held the man: "Everybody here Agrees in A contemptible Opinion of Cosby & no body knows him better or has A worse Opinion of him than the friends he relies on." Yet Morris still worried that Cosby's station as a colonial governor, and his close ties, through marriage, to members of the Council, would insulate him from rebuke and removal. "It may be you will be surprised to hear that the most Nefarious crime A governour can commit is not by Some counted so bad as the crime of Complaining of it," he wrote to Alexander, "the last is an arraigning of the ministry that advis'd the Sending of him, Exposing them to censure and by doing so Exciting the people to clamour and weakening the hands of the government."

A member of an Anglo-Irish military family, Cosby had joined the British army at age fourteen and had risen over time to the rank of Colonel of the Royal Regiment of Ireland. At Menorca, in Spain's Balearic Islands, he had served for ten years as royal governor before being assigned a post in the Leeward Islands of the West Indies in the Caribbean Sea. Then, in 1732, his wife's cousin, the Duke of Newcastle, handpicked him to be the royal governor of New York. There his high-handed treatment of the American colonists almost immediately made him unpopular. Aside from their aggravation at his supercilious demeanor, many New Yorkers were aware of Cosby's reputation in Spain for greed and self-dealing in office. As one contemporary political opponent described him, "[Cosby] recv'd [New Yorkers] with all the affected Spanish Gravity which, it may be supposed, he had acquired and practiced at Port Mahon, for which people began to think that he intended to use the same kind of Government over the English here that he had over the conquer'd Spanish there."

According to one New Yorker active in colonial politics, "No representation repugnant to his avarice had any influence upon Mr. Cosby." He was particularly notorious for an episode in Menorca in which he tried to illegally appropriate a load of snuff from a Portuguese merchant. The affair had left Cosby heavily indebted, and many of his new subjects in America suspected that he had sought the position in New York only because of its potential for greater remuneration than he had enjoyed in the Caribbean.

Whether or not this was an accurate account of Cosby's motives, it was all too fitting that one of the governor's first actions after arriving in New York was to sue another government official for a portion of that official's salary. That other official was Rip Van Dam, a Dutchman from Albany, who, upon the death of Cosby's predecessor, John Montgomerie, had served as acting governor of New York. Cosby claimed he was entitled to half the salary paid to Van Dam as acting governor, and, when Van Dam refused to oblige, Cosby attempted to bring suit in New York's colonial court system.

Viewed in terms of its consequences, Cosby's decision was a calamitous one. Yet at the time it was surely difficult for Cosby to foresee the political turmoil that his suit against Van Dam would create. After all, if a royal governor of an English colony was not able to use his public position for private gain, so the thinking probably went, what was the point of being all the way across the Atlantic? But Cosby badly miscalculated the strength of the political opposition he would face in New York, and his simple act of venality created an uproar that would not subside until his death in office four years later.

As events rapidly unfolded, Cosby's lawsuit, *King v. Van Dam*, spiraled out of the governor's control. One of his chief political opponents, Lewis Morris, sitting as chief justice of New York's supreme court, read from the bench a lengthy opinion that rejected the legal theory under which Cosby proceeded against Van Dam. Morris's opinion infuriated Cosby, and when Morris later published it in a New York newspaper, Cosby responded to this public slight by summarily removing Morris from his post. Morris's removal, in turn, sparked the formation of a new political party opposing the governor and his policies. In effect, what had started as a simple case of gubernatorial avarice turned into a referendum on judicial independence and the rule of law. And it was the strength of the opposition to Cosby in New York that gave Morris, waiting to be heard in London in 1735, confidence in his mission.

That Cosby had arrived at his position in New York through a system of colonial patronage was beyond dispute. His brother-in-law was the influential Charles Montagu, 1st Earl of Halifax, who was a member of George II's Privy Council. Cosby was also related through marriage to Thomas Pelham-Holles, 1st Duke of Newcastle-upon-Tyne, who was also 1st Duke of Newcastle-under-Lyne and was a dispenser of colonial patronage par excellence. With Cosby backed by these powerful forces in England, his conduct was difficult to check, and Morris risked, and ultimately lost, his position on the supreme court by trying to check it. But in deciding whether to challenge Cosby's lawlessness, it had to help that Morris was a prominent man whose political fortunes had recently declined. He was also the resolute, independent-minded man who set out for the Caribbean at eighteen and by nineteen was one of the largest landowners in New York. He had little to lose and much to gain if he could mount a successful challenge to an unpopular royal governor. And so Lewis Morris decided to rebuff the governor's attempted end-run around the common-law courts.

A Typical Landed Aristocrat

At first blush, Lewis Morris looks like an unlikely champion for the cause of judicial independence. Allegedly descended from Welsh nobility, he was born in 1671 to a landed family of colonial merchants. Morris's estate, located in what is now Bronx County, New York, was named Morrisania, an obvious sign of the family's dynastic sensibilities. Having lost his parents in his first year of life, Morris received a vast inheritance from his uncle at the age of nineteen. In addition to Morrisania, he gained sizable tracts of land in New Jersey and Long Island as well as a home in New York City. In addition, through advantageous litigation of his aunt's will, he inherited what was surely a stupendous fortune for a young man of the time. After coming into this inheritance, he obtained for Morrisania the status of a manor and for himself the rights of a manorial lord. African slaves worked his land. Indeed, by some accounts Morris was the largest slaveholder in New York and New Jersey. In these respects, Morris was a typical landed aristocrat of the American colonial period. He was certainly not a democrat in any sense of the term. As Morris's biographer, Eugene R. Sheridan, described him, ". . . he was a dedicated elitist who believed as a matter of course that his wealth and social standing gave him the right to act as one of society's natural leaders and to be recognized as such by common people, fellow aristocrats, and imperial officials alike. . . . Morris deduced that those who had the greatest material stake in society should have the largest say in the direction of its political affairs." And while land and great wealth gave Morris a sense of natural superiority perhaps inconsistent with the democratic ideals usually associated with the rule of law, his status provided him with the financial and social independence to challenge a man in Cosby's position.

Morris possessed other qualities that prepared him for his role in the struggle for judicial independence. One such quality was ambition. From a young age, he seemed to have an unabated desire to rise to prominence in public life—a desire that, along with the skill and experience he subsequently gained in his long political career, made him a formidable opponent to Governor Cosby.

Morris relied on his several estates to provide the income and sustenance needed to support his family, for, in contrast to his uncle, he eschewed business as a merchant. He distrusted merchants and thought their dealings shabby and beneath a true gentleman. Consistent with this view, he believed his status as a wealthy landholder made him uniquely fit for political life, and from an early age he vigorously pursued a political career.

Apart from providing a steady stream of income, the landed

gentry were a powerful political faction in colonial politics, and as a fellow aristocrat, Morris wasted no time in assuming public office by exploiting his status. Following in his uncle's footsteps (politically, if not commercially), he entered the East Jersey Council and Court of Common Right in 1692. He was twenty years old. For the next fifteen years, he was primarily involved in the politics of New Jersey, where he played an instrumental role in returning power over the colonial government to the crown. By thirty-six, he was president of the New Jersey Council.

Throughout this time, Morris was alternately in and out of favor with New Jersey's various governors. Twice his strident criticism of the corrupt administration of Lord Cornbury, the first royal governor of the combined provinces of New York and New Jersey, led Cornbury to dismiss him from the governor's council. (In the British peerage system, Lord Cornbury was a courtesy title for Edward Hyde, Viscount Cornbury.) Appointed governor by his cousin, Queen Anne, Cornbury was an unruly despot indifferent to the needs of his people. The critical Morris considered him "a wretch who by the whole conduct of his life has evidenced he has no regard for honor or virtue."

Turning from the governor's council to elective politics, at age thity-nine Morris joined the New York assembly. Once there, he was able to successfully petition Queen Anne for Cornbury's recall. This early experience in opposing the crown's representative in the colonies undoubtedly helped steel Morris's resolve when confronting Cosby in the 1730s.

In 1715, Morris's friend and ally Robert Hunter (governor of New Jersey and of New York from 1710 to 1720 and notably one of the few royal governors with whom Morris had a truly amicable relationship) appointed the forty-three-year-old to be chief justice of the supreme court of New York, a position he would hold for nearly twenty years, until Cosby removed him in 1733. Thus, by the time of Cosby's arrival, Morris was one of the most experienced politicians in the colony. Moreover, he was a man who was not easily cowed by the bluster of a royal governor.

To further his political ambition, Morris tried to gain a store of knowledge matching his high station in life. Like many prominent men in the New World, he was self-taught. Having received little formal education in his youth, as an adult he became a voracious reader. He studied Latin, Greek, Hebrew, and Arabic, and he immersed himself in the classical works of the late Roman Republic.

Throughout his life, Morris was attentive to the political debates of the day. In the early 1720s, when John Trenchard and Thomas Gordon published *Cato's Letters*, a series of 144 essays condemning corruption and immorality within the British political system, Morris read with interest their whiggish defense of individual liberty. He wrote poetry, taught himself to play the fiddle, and frequently published editorials in New York newspapers. In short, Morris was a product of the seventeenth-century Enlightenment, which, among other things, considered a breadth of learning *de rigueur* for country gentlemen.

Although Morris was a well-informed and politically conscious aristocrat, perhaps more important in his struggle against Cosby's exercise of arbitrary power was a different facet of his personality: his strident independence. Having lost his parents before his first birthday, Morris, in order to survive, had developed an independent streak. While a series of aunts and uncles provided for him, his disruptive early years left him, as biographer Sherman wrote, a "defiant, high-spirited, rebellious child." What few traits Lewis's father, Richard Morris, may have imparted to his son were likely to have only reinforced the young man's boldness.

Richard Morris himself was a rebel. He took up a sword for the parliamentary faction in the English Civil War, resisting the absolutist rule of Charles I. After the king was beheaded and Oliver

Cromwell was installed as head of the commonwealth, Captain Morris set out to join his older brother's business in Barbados. There he married Lewis's mother, Sarah, and in 1670 moved with her to New York. Shortly after purchasing the land that would eventually become Morrisania, both Richard and Sarah Morris died, and Lewis was left alone in the New World. The toddler had a series of guardians in the two years following his parents' death.

Lewis Morris's young life finally gained some semblance of stability when his uncle, also named Lewis Morris, became his namesake's guardian. Morris was only three years old at the time, but the rebellious tendencies produced by his tumultuous early years were firmly in place. To be sure, the flinty Quakerism of his septuagenarian uncle only aggravated the boy's natural stubbornness. Apparently, young Morris also chafed under the rule of his uncle's wife, Mary, an erstwhile maid several years junior to her husband. (Morris family lore accuses Mary of keeping the boy at arm's length so as to cut off any inheritance he might otherwise receive from his uncle.) And despite his uncle's devout commitment to the Quaker faith, Morris resisted the religion throughout his upbringing—going so far as to play pranks on the Quaker tutors the elder Morris hired to educate his nephew. To hide from one tutor, the adult Morris later recalled, he hid in a hollowed-out tree, where he impersonated a divine voice commanding his overly credulous instructor to bring the Lord's gospel to the heathen Mohawk of upstate New York.

Whether Morris's disobedience soured relations with his uncle or the relationship was strained for other reasons, at the age of eighteen Morris decided to strike out on his own. He traveled over land from New York to Virginia. From there, perhaps inspired by his father's fortunes, he set sail for the Caribbean, where he worked in Jamaica as a scrivener—a professional copyist or scribe. Of course, many young men grew up quickly in that era, but the fact that the scion of a wealthy, landed family chose to forgo the possibility of an ample inheritance for the uncertainty of an independent life is a testament to the youth's self-assurance and resolve.

Morris's time as a scrivener was short-lived. Almost exactly one year after the young Lewis set out to find his own way, his uncle tracked him down and brought him back to New York. Then, in what was most likely felicitous timing for the disaffected young man, his uncle and aunt died within a month of his return. For the second time, Morris had lost his two parental figures (and no matter how much he disliked Lewis and Mary Morris, that's what they were) in the span of a week. However, the generous bequest of his uncle and the litigated will of his aunt made the impetuous youth one of the most prominent landed aristocrats in New York and New Jersey. His marriage the following year to Isabella Graham, daughter of New York's attorney general, further solidified his position as one of the leading men in the colony. And while the rebelliousness of youth may have mellowed as Morris gained age and responsibility, the chief justice of the New York Supreme Court exhibited an unmistakable streak of independent thought and action in his fight against Governor Cosby. It could be said fairly that the sixty-three-year-old man who sailed to England to press his case in 1734 was, in many ways, not unlike the independent-minded eighteen-year-old who had sailed to Jamaica in 1690.

Avoiding a Jury Trial

Governor Cosby faced a dilemma: He did not know where to bring his suit against Rip Van Dam. Given his negative reputation among New Yorkers, he believed a local jury was likely to decide the matter in favor of the local Dutchman, who, after all, had served the colony in satisfactory fashion before Cosby arrived. That meant that if he wanted to increase his chances of recovering from Van Dam, Cosby would need to avoid bringing his suit in New York's common-law courts, which required jury trials. Unfortunately for Cosby, pursuing his claim in chancery posed problems as well because, while the equity courts were a juryless forum, Cosby's position as governor meant that he was also chancellor for the colony. This, in turn, meant that he would be required to be a judge in his own case in the Court of Chancery. Equity law, however, prohibited such a result, so Cosby seemed to be forced back into the law courts if he wanted to proceed against Van Dam. But the man was a creative schemer. He issued letters patent instructing the justices from the colony's supreme court to sit as a special court of the exchequer. He could then bring his suit against Van Dam on this special court's equity side, where no jury trial would be necessary.

The creation of this hybrid tribunal—a court of the exchequer comprised of supreme court personnel—would allow Cosby to avoid the vagaries of a jury trial in the law courts while also not forcing him to create an entirely new court to hear his case. It would also alleviate the difficulties posed by equity law in the Court of Chancery. For Cosby, an added attraction of this arrangement (and one he was surely aware of) was that the supreme court justices trying his case held their judicial posts at the pleasure of the royal governor. Thus Cosby's "solution" to the problem of suing Van Dam was, as one historian surmised from contemporary correspondence, "an alarming portent that the governor made 'Little Distinction betwixt power and right' in his determination to maximize the profits of his office."

The three supreme court justices whom Cosby instructed to sit as a special court for the Van Dam case were Lewis Morris, James DeLancey, and Frederick Philipse. The latter two were partisans of Cosby ("Cosbyites"), and Morris knew that no matter what their views of the propriety of the proceedings, DeLancey and Philipse were unlikely to rule against the man who held their careers in the balance. Morris, on the other hand, felt no particular fealty to

Cosby. If anything, Cosby was a natural political opponent who had aligned himself with Morris's enemies in New York politics. In addition, Cosby's attempt to obtain monies paid to Van Dam in his capacity as acting governor of the colony imperiled Morris's own finances. Morris had acted as chief executive for New Jersey after Governor Montgomerie's death, just as Van Dam had served in that capacity in New York, so a ruling in favor of Cosby would have put Morris's own salary and emoluments from that period in jeopardy. But whatever Morris's financial stake in the outcome, his sense of the rule of law was deeply offended by Cosby's actions, for Cosby was effectively trying to deprive Van Dam of his right to a trial by jury. He was doing so by using his power as governor to manipulate the colonial court system; not satisfied with removing the matter from consideration by a jury, Cosby imposed his inherent authority over the justices of the supreme court to ensure a favorable result. Such a gross and flagrant abuse of power only confirmed fears that Cosby was an unprincipled beneficiary of political patronage who had no interest in legitimate governance.

Why Cosby Removed Morris from Office

Cosby's suit against Van Dam went before the special session of the supreme court on March 14, 1733. Morris began by dropping a bomb on the proceedings: Before hearing arguments on the merits, he asked the attorneys for both sides to address the question of the supreme court's (now the exchequer court's) equity jurisdiction. Counsel for Van Dam, in their pleadings to the court, had argued against its jurisdiction in the case, and in particular had argued that a royal governor had no power, absent legislative approval, to establish an exchequer court to hear cases in equity. Now Morris was asking both sides to limit their arguments to this narrow point.

Counsel for the crown was caught off guard and objected to the form of argument requested by Chief Justice Morris. This objection being overruled, the crown proceeded to argue in favor of equity jurisdiction in the exchequer court. We have no record of the actual arguments, but based on the materials prepared beforehand by counsel for the crown, we can surmise that their argument focused on the constitutional status of the court of the exchequer in Great Britain. Because that court was established by custom and common law, its equity jurisdiction did not rely on a commission from Parliament. And because the American colonists were entitled to the same laws enjoyed by Englishmen living at home, so the crown's argument probably went, the exchequer court in New York should also be understood as a creature of English common law, and should require no more legislative sanction than its counterpart in Britain.

Van Dam's lawyers, most likely apprised of Morris's opening question beforehand, were better prepared. They relied on no less authority than Lord Coke—i.e., Sir Edward Coke, Lord Chief Justice of England, 1613 to 1616, whose legal writings had staunchly defended the rule of law vis-a-vis royal absolutism—for the proposition that the king could not establish a court of equity without the consent of the legislature. They acknowledged that the court of the exchequer was not founded on an act of Parliament, but they argued that it had developed contemporaneously with the English Constitution and had been subsequently ratified by various acts of Parliament. They agreed with counsel for the crown that the colonists were guaranteed all the benefits of English law, but they argued that the proposition cut the other way. In particular, Van Dam's counsel argued, the colonists were entitled to the benefit of the laws abolishing courts of equity that were not founded on prescription or act of Parliament. They further cited a series of previous resolutions made by the general assembly of New York to the effect that Cosby's decision to create a new court of equity was "without precedent, inconvenient, and contrary to the laws of England."

Morris had researched the issue in advance of the hearing (in fact, it has been suggested that he went so far as to confer with Van Dam's lawyers, who were also his political allies—a clear breach of judicial impartiality, if true). His opinion of the law was that New York's supreme court, even when constituted as a court of the exchequer, could not hear equity cases. More importantly, his research had convinced him that neither the governor nor the provincial council was permitted to establish an exchequer court to hear equity cases without legislative approval, meaning that the general assembly of New York had to sign off. Immediately following the arguments by counsel and without leaving the bench (as was customary), he read a prepared opinion denying the court's jurisdiction to hear the case. Thus, by challenging the authority of a royal governor to tamper with the colonial court system, he offered a powerful defense of judicial independence from executive interference.

Morris began his opinion by acknowledging what he perceived to be some general truths concerning the law of the case. The most important of these was that, no matter how unfettered the king was in his use of the royal prerogative in the provinces, the justices of the supreme court were bound to judge each case according to the laws of England. In essence, this meant that the king's free hand in making policy for the American colonies did not allow the colonial judges to ignore the laws of Parliament and the English Constitution. Morris then posed four questions:

1. Under English law, does the king possess the power to erect courts of equity by letters patent (i.e., exclusive of the legislature)?
2. Under English law, has the king given Governor Cosby such a power?
3. Has there been erected, under any law, a court of the exchequer (considered as a court of equity) in New York?

4. Is there any less authority than the whole general assembly of New York that is permitted to erect a court of equity?

Through an assiduous, point-by-point analysis of precedent, Morris answered each of these questions in the negative. Given those answers, his conclusion was unambiguous: "And therefore upon the whole it seems plain to me, that we neither have, or ever had, or ever were intended to have, any Jurisdiction in a Court of Equity; nor can such a Jurisdiction by any Letters Patent or Ordinance, not founded on an Act of the Legislature, be given. . . . And therefore by the Grace of God, I, as chief Justice of this Province, shall not pay any Obedience to them in that Point."

The two junior justices, not having been made aware of Morris's plans, took longer to formulate their opinions. Five days after Chief Justice Morris had read his opinion from the bench, Justice DeLancey announced that in his opinion the supreme court possessed power to hear pleas in equity. It was not until the following term that Justice Philipse delivered his opinion, and he sided with DeLancey. The following day, Morris (who had been absent from the bench when Philipse delivered his opinion) excoriated his junior colleagues, calling their opinions "mean, weak, and futile." Then, to the astonishment of onlookers, he stalked off and refused to return while the court sat over any equity case. While as a practical matter Morris's departure from the bench ended the *King v. Van Dam* suit, the larger confrontation with Cosby was hardly over.

Governor Cosby did not take the news of Morris's opinion well. After it was announced, he angrily refused to receive Morris, saying that he could "neither rely upon [Morris's] integrity nor depend upon his judgment or opinion" and that Morris had treated him "with Slight, Rudenesse, and Impertinence" ever since he arrived at the colony as the king's representative. Somewhat taken aback by Cosby's rage, Morris perhaps expected that his removal from the supreme court was simply a matter of time.

Later in March, Cosby demanded a copy of Morris's opinion in *King v. Van Dam*. Morris obliged, somewhat rashly, by publishing his opinion in a pamphlet by a young German immigrant named John Peter Zenger. (The story of Cosby's later efforts to silence Zenger's paper is too long to tell here, but again Cosby used his preferred tactic of attempting to stack the judicial proceedings in his favor. The two-man court created to preside over the Zenger trial consisted of none other than James DeLancey and Frederick Philipse, the two other members of Morris's panel on the exchequer court.)

Morris's opinion in the *Van Dam* case, accompanied by an open letter from the chief justice to the governor, was distributed throughout the colony. The letter began by reciting the language Cosby had used earlier in the month to rebuff Morris. It went on to apologize for moving the governor to such "a great degree of Warmth," but reminded him that he was merely "giving [his] Opinion in a Court of which [he] was a Judge, on a Point of Law, that came before [him]." Then, taking Cosby's conduct head-on, he wrote to the governor:

> Judges are no more infallible than their Superiors are impeccable: But if Judges are to be intimidated so as not to dare give any Opinion but what is pleasing to a Governour, and agreeable to his Private views, the People of this Province, who are very much concern'd both with Respect to their Lives and Fortunes in the Freedom and Independency of those who are to Judge them, may possibly not think themselves so secure in either of them as the Laws and his Majesty intends they should be.

For Cosby, it was the last straw. In August 1733 he summarily dismissed Morris from his position as chief justice. He did not consult the provincial council before doing so, and he gave no reason for his decision. He then quickly promoted Delancey to chief justice and moved Philipse to second justice, thereby shoring up support from the Cosbyite judges. But the governor's ham-fisted dismissal of Morris made the political nature of his decision transparent.

Assembly Seat and Alert Public

Morris was out of public office for the first time in twenty years, but his political fortunes were once again on the rise. By removing him without explanation or consultation, Cosby inadvertently turned him into a popular hero and the natural leader of the "country party," the opposition to Cosby's "court party." The public perception in New York, accurately reflecting reality, was that Cosby had removed Morris from his position as chief justice because he had found Morris's opinion in the Van Dam case so disagreeable. Morris described Cosby's decision to remove him in a letter to the Board of Trade later that same month: "The reasons for displacing a judge Should (in my humble Opinion) be not only in themselves verry good, but verry evident; nothing being more distastfull than the arbitrary removal of Judges. . . . I cannot tell what occasioned [Cosby's] difference with me unlesse it was an Opinion I gave on a matter in judgement before me." Although perhaps deliberately naïve in speculating on the reasons for his ouster, Morris was appealing to a shared sentiment at the time: Judges should not be subject to arbitrary removal. It was Cosby's flagrant violation of this principle, in addition to his personal unpopularity, that allowed Morris and his allies to mount an effective opposition to the governor's "court party."

Soon after his dismissal, Morris ran for an open assembly seat in Westchester. His opponent was William Forster, the candidate favored by Cosby's "court party." Despite vocal opposition mounted by his former colleagues DeLancey and Philipse, Morris won the race by a sizable margin. An anecdote from the Westchester election nicely captures the conflicting tendencies in Morris's personality. In a colorful contest, the candidates, led by musicians and followed by throngs of supporters, rode around the village green. The local sheriff, however, who was a partisan of Governor Cosby, tried to tip the scales in favor of Morris's opponent. Alleging that a number of Quaker supporters of the former chief justice would not swear that they satisfied the property requirements that could make them eligible to vote, the sheriff disqualified them. Morris and his supporters were outraged.

After Morris's victory was announced, his opponent attempted reconciliation, but Morris would have none of it. He called Forster "highly blamable" for the sheriff's conduct, which to Morris's eyes amounted to a "violent . . . attempt upon the Liberty of the People." Upon hearing their champion rebuff Forster, Morris's supporters gave an enthusiastic cheer, but, true to his aristocratic sensibilities, Morris "reproved them for making such an unseemly display." Thus, in one verbal altercation, we see both sides of Morris: He was an uncompromising supporter of electoral rights (such as they were at the time) and of the rule of law, but he was nevertheless an elitist who considered himself superior to the electorate that had just handed him a much-needed victory.

Around the same time, Morris was serving the country party's cause in a second capacity as one of the chief contributors to Peter Zenger's *New York Weekly Journal*. Zenger's newspaper was both an organ for criticism of Cosby's administration and a voice for greater independence in the judiciary. Despite the long history of judges sitting at the pleasure of provincial governors, the *Journal* began openly advocating that judgeships be created by statute and that judges be allowed to serve for terms in good behavior.

According to one historian, with these demands, "Morris and the country party expressed a deep-seated desire of politically aware New Yorkers to apply English legal precedents to their province, so that thereby they could share more fully in the rights and privileges of Englishmen."

The *Van Dam* case and Cosby's subsequent dismissal of Morris alerted the public to the incredible influence that colonial governors exerted over judges. The simple fact that Governor Cosby could not have played the same games with the courts back home in England struck many New Yorkers as fundamentally unfair. Why should colonists have to suffer the rapacity of provincial governors while Englishmen enjoyed the rule of law and the protection of their property by an independent judiciary? An ideological consensus was forming among the leaders of the country party and the readers of the *Journal*, and it was an ideology opposed to vesting unchecked and arbitrary power in provincial governors. Cosby's brazen attempts to circumvent jury trials, intimidate judges, and silence public criticism of his actions demonstrated how perilous the rule of law was in a system lacking judicial independence.

Cosby Not Removed, But a Governorship Gained

It was near the end of 1735 when Lewis Morris was finally admitted to the King's Privy Council. Despite his confidence that he would achieve both Cosby's removal and his own restoration to the supreme court, Morris failed to gain either result. The issue of Cosby's removal was mooted by his death in March of 1736. But even before the news of his death reached England, the Privy Council had shown little interest in removing a provincial governor who enjoyed the support of important figures in Walpolean England.

A majority of the Privy Council agreed that Morris's dismissal was unwarranted and that Cosby had acted wrongly in removing

him, but the counselors stopped short of recommending his rein-
statement. Instead, after many rounds of back-channel negotiation,
he was persuaded to take, as a consolation prize, the governorship
of the newly formed independent province of New Jersey. While
he had been unable to achieve his immediate goals, his mission was
not, however, entirely in vain: From the Privy Council he gained
partial vindication, and his political fortunes were buoyed by the
promise of a new post.

Morris was a complex man, and his opposition to Cosby was
motivated as much by personal ambition as by principle. There can
be no doubt that he was perfectly happy to use his judicial platform in *King v. Van Dam* to frustrate his chief political opponent.
And since there was too much at stake for him personally in the
outcome of his dispute with Cosby, he is not the purest example of
judicial courage in the face of executive encroachment. There is also
the lingering question of his unethical behavior throughout this
episode. It is argued, and perhaps quite likely, that Morris tipped
off Van Dam's counsel about his initial question at the hearing.
Moreover, in what looked like a childish fit of pique, Morris left
the bench after being confronted by the contrary opinion of a col-
league who was a junior justice—an opinion Morris denounced as
"futile." Apart from making him look like a sore loser, his absence
effectively terminated a case he did not want to hear.

Morris's ideological commitments are no less open to question
than his judicial ethics. He was, after all, a slaveholding aristocrat
who had spent much of his career defending the royal prerogative
when it suited him. Indeed, the most damning evidence in this
regard came after the affair with Cosby and during Morris's tenure
as governor of New Jersey. Taking the post at the age of sixty-six,
he quickly abandoned his role as "country party" maverick and
became a staunch conservative defender of the royal prerogative
and the crown's interests. By the time he died, in fact, he was so

unpopular with the New Jersey Assembly that the legislature, which as governor he had dissolved several times, refused to pay his family the remainder of his salary. Thus Morris was, in many respects, a political opportunist throughout his career, and the *Van Dam* case was certainly no exception. But in the last analysis, the principles and ideas he drew upon in opposing Cosby were real, and he firmly believed in them. Indeed, his opinion in the *Van Dam* case was not a cynical effort to use constitutional arguments to score political points. Rather, in that case his political interests intersected with a profound constitutional dispute, and he was able to use his skills as both a politician and a lawyer to combat a venal and corrupt representative of the crown.

Beyond Morris's own story, the fallout from *King v. Van Dam* changed popular attitudes toward colonial governance. Cosby's naked attempt to manipulate New York's courts and judges for his own ends highlighted the distinction between the rights enjoyed by the American colonists and those enjoyed by their English counterparts. The experience in New York with such governors as Cosby (and such subservient colonial judges as DeLancey and Philipse) made many people realize that the rule of law required an independent judiciary. In 1787, some fifty-four years after Cosby dismissed Lewis Morris from New York's supreme court, Morris's grandson Gouverneur Morris represented the state of New York at the Constitutional Convention in Philadelphia. There can be little doubt that memories of men like William Cosby were fresh in the minds of the delegates when they guaranteed in Article III that judges would be sufficiently independent to check the abuse of power and safeguard our liberty.

3

The People's Court in Nazi Germany

Under a government which imprisons any unjustly, the true place for a just man is in prison.

—Henry David Thoreau

It is dangerous to be right when the government is wrong.

—Voltaire

IN GERMANY IN 1942, SOPHIE SCHOLL WAS A VIBRANT TWENTY-one-year-old, sailing through that time in her life when curiosity is irrepressible and free thought and free speech are paramount. Unfortunately, Sophie was growing up in one of the most stiflingly repressive environments in history—in a society governed by the edicts of Adolf Hitler. Non-conforming speech was then instantly and brutally smothered, for all Germans were expected to support Hitler's principles, in thought and deed. Despite dim prospects for the future, Sophie's parents hoped for the best. Their daughter had always found a way to succeed, to rise to the top, to accomplish her objectives. This time would be no different.

During the 1930s, the German rule of law began a precipitous decline that closely tracked, unsurprisingly, the rise of the National Socialist German Workers' Party—the Nazis. Early in 1930, they won a ninefold increase in parliamentary seats over the 1928

Reichstag elections. That was enough to give them significant influence in the government. Hitler, the leader of the party and newly appointed chancellor, convened his top advisers and deputies—Rudolf Hess, Joseph Goebbels, Heinrich Himmler, and Hermann Göring—to take advantage of the new public support by starting an aggressive campaign of propaganda and destabilization. Exercising characteristic doublespeak, Hitler openly purported to respect and nurture the law, while in reality he harbored deep resentment and sought only to dismantle existing legal structures and remake the judiciary as he pleased. In 1933, in his first speech as chancellor, he declared: "We [will] rebuild our *Volk* not according to theories hatched by some alien brain, but according to the eternal laws valid for all time." Paradoxically, the "theories hatched by some alien brain" were the laws promulgated by the proper authority through the proper process and adjudicated by the proper authorities, while "the eternal laws valid for all time" were the arbitrary principles Hitler chose to implement.

The Beginning of the End

In 1933, the Reichstag fire incident, during which the house of the new German Parliament burned to the ground, consummated the decline of the rule of law and snuffed out its last breath. A young man named Marinus van der Lubbe, who was a Dutch Communist and recent German immigrant known for being critical of the new Nazi government, was quickly convicted of arson and executed. Despite van der Lubbe's insistence throughout his interrogation and trial that the German communist political party, the KPD, was not involved in the plan to burn the Reichstag, police arrested four prominent Communist leaders for allegedly conspiring with van der Lubbe. The Reichsgericht, the highest court of the German Empire in Leipzig, however, acquitted all four men. Hitler was outraged. He lashed out at the judiciary. It was the beginning of the end for an independent judiciary in Germany.

In 1934, in what became known as the Night of the Long Knives, Hitler kicked off the new year by purging political opponents. At a public rally, during a speech that provided a window into his warped conception of judges and the law, he defended his actions:

> If anyone reproaches me and asks why we did not call upon the regular courts for sentencing, my only answer is this: in that hour, I was responsible for the fate of the German nation and was thus the Supreme Judge of the *German Volk* . . . When people confront me with the view that only a trial in court would have been capable of accurately weighing the measure of guilt ad expiation, I must lodge a solemn protest. He who rises up against Germany commits treason. He who commits treason is to be punished not according to the scope and proportions of his deed, but rather according to his case of mind as revealed therein.

In a baffling string of non-sequiturs, Hitler essentially explained away the need for an independent judiciary: He knew treason when he saw it, and he could intuit *mens rea*—the guilty mind—from the fact of the treasonous act. In Hitler's conception, judges, without discretion of their own, were merely administrators of the executive's precepts.

"The People's Court" Is Hitler's Court

Based on these principles, Hitler took action. First, he established the Volksgerichtshof, or "People's Court." Rather than serving the people, however, the People's Court represented only the interests of Hitler and the National Socialists. Next, he pushed the passage of the Enabling Law, which greatly expanded his plenary powers and allowed the executive to pass laws and budgets and even modify the constitution. Articles Two and Three of the act were the most potent, providing that the chancellor could unilaterally enact laws, and that those laws could deviate from the constitution. Either one of Hitler's actions would have been cause for alarm. Together, they were utterly devastating. The Enabling Law allowed Hitler to promulgate any law he wished, and the People's Court judges, in the pocket of the Führer, would ensure that his edicts and brutal "justice" were carried out swiftly. Hitler kept the judges close by using the new Law for the Restoration of the Professional Civil Service—unsurprisingly, another misnomer, since the law required judges to approach cases with "a healthy prejudice" and rule in line with "the main principles of the Führer's government." In addition, the law allowed the government to terminate not only political opponents but also tenured government workers who were not of Aryan descent.

Immediately after he passed the restoration law, Hitler began clearing the judiciary of Jewish judges, judges unsympathetic to the Nazi philosophy, and judges who refused to bow unquestioningly to executive pressure. He appointed partisan judges, who were, according to Volksgerichtshof vice president Karl Engert, "politicians first and judges second." Even then, Hitler constrained the new judges by removing jurisdictions and making new law whenever he pleased.

The new system required prosecutors not to pursue justice or serve the people, but, in the words of one senior prosecutor, to "annihilate the enemies of national socialism." The resultant distorted creature was a justice system in name only; the People's Court spewed injustice, inequity, and prejudice.

After Hitler solidified his power and dismantled the independent judiciary, he was free to begin his savage agenda for depopulation and social engineering. He proclaimed a panoply of laws, including laws allowing the government to arbitrarily label citizens as habitual criminals and permitting even more severe punishments, including castration and indefinite detention in asylums or workhouses. Further laws regulated the practice of law and outlawed opposing political views. By the time war broke out, Hitler and the Nazi party had virtually complete control over the legal system—both legislative and adjudicative. On April 26, 1942, Hitler informed the Reichstag that he would have exclusive control over the tenure of the judiciary:

I do expect one thing: that the nation gives me the right to intervene immediately and to take action myself whenever a person has failed to render unqualified obedience . . . I therefore ask the German Reichstag to confirm expressly that I have the legal right to keep everybody to his duty and to cashier or remove from office or position without regard for his person or his established rights, whoever, in my view and according to my considered opinion, has failed to do his duty. . . . From now on, I shall intervene in these cases and remove from office those judges who evidently do not understand the demand of the hour.

Predictably, the Reichstag confirmed Hitler's "request" and resolved that:

The Führer must have all the rights postulated by him which serve to further or achieve victory. Therefore—without being bound by existing legal regulations—in his capacity as leader of the nation, Supreme Commander of the Armed Forces, governmental chief and supreme executive chief, as supreme justice, and leader of the Party—the Führer must be in a position to force with all means at his disposal every German, if necessary, whether he be common soldier or officer, low or high official or judge, leading or subordinate official of the Party, worker or employee, to fulfill his duties. In case of violation of these duties, the Führer is entitled after conscientious examination, regardless of so-called well-deserved rights, to mete out due punishment, and to remove the offender from his post, rank and position, without introducing prescribed procedures.

Essentially, Hitler captured the power of an emperor. Like Louis XIV, he was rendered *legibus solutus*, or above the law.

Hitlerjugen and Bund Deutscher Mädel

Unfortunately it was in this environment in Hitler's Germany that Sophie Scholl and her older brother, Hans, and younger sister, Inge, reached their formative years. Growing up in Ulm, in the westernmost part of Germany, Sophie was eleven years old when the Nazis seized power. She and her siblings were quickly funneled into the Hitlerjugen (Hitler's Youth) and the BDM—the Bund Deutscher Mädel—the girls' equivalent of the Youth. These were the Führer's programs for grooming German boys and girls into compliant, lockstep citizens of the Third Reich.

Robert Scholl—father of Sophie, Inge, and Hans—was a liberal humanist who vehemently opposed the changes implemented by the National Socialists. His children, however, were being programmed to value nationalism above all else—even family bonds and education. Arguments broke out frequently over dinner, with Robert decrying the Nazis as wild beasts and abusive wolves while his swastika-emblazoned son sat and stewed.

Hans was progressing faster than most in the Nazi-grooming apparatus. He was appointed Fähnleinführer, or group leader, of a 150–boy squad of the Hitler Youth, which set him up for a future position of authority in the government, most likely a leadership position in the SS. Before long, however, his fervor began to wane. As a young man who was a creative, non-conformist attention-seeker, he found the cog-in-the-wheel mentality of the program starting to eat away at his nature. For example, he was warned against singing the Russian folk tunes he enjoyed playing on his guitar for his classmates. Later, he was harshly repudiated for reading one of his favorite books, a historical tome of man's achievements, because its author was Stefan Zweig, a Jew. Perhaps, too, Robert Scholl's seeds had begun to take root in Hans. His home was a haven for open-minded thought and diverse education. His parents' Jewish friends still came to visit on weekends, and multi-cultural music and books comprised the evening entertainment.

By the time he was given the honor of carrying a banner in Hitler's 1936 rally in Nuremburg, where four hundred thousand gathered, chanted, and deified the Nazi leader, Hans had grown to resent the party and its values. Standing among the masses, he realized that individuality, creativity, and diversity would be casualties of the Nazi agenda. Shortly thereafter, he was demoted before his entire brigade for marching under a banner portraying a griffin— his own design—and assaulting a superior officer who tried to strip the banner from the hands of a member of his squad. Hans had now had enough of the Hitler's Youth, and he determined to reverse the course on which he found himself. He and other disillusioned young men were learning that despite service in the Youth, which was compulsory, they could pursue very different and potentially treasonous second lives.

Meanwhile, Sophie and Inge, following in their brother's footsteps as usual, had become involved in the BDM. Sophie's primary interest was not the group's political implications but rather its camping, hiking, and camaraderie. However, around the time Hans's interest in the Youth waned, Sophie, too, was becoming disillusioned with the BDM. Under the pleasant social aspects of the group, she realized, lay a hidden agenda—to transform young women into Hitler's vision of the perfect Aryan female, which she saw as a regressive, stiflingly traditional view. The girls were increasingly expected to fit a narrow, antiquated pattern that would have them cooking meals, wearing braids, and bearing strong Aryan children, without room for nonconforming aspirations for lifestyle or careers. Sophie loved diverse literature, wrote poetry, had a sharp, independent mind, and dreamed of going to university in Munich. None of these plans and characteristics fit into the Führer's vision of womanhood.

Once the Scholl children began to distance themselves from their compelled Nazi indoctrination, the household became, once again, a haven for tolerance, intellectualism, and open-minded discussion. Robert Scholl had recalled his children from the Führer's grasp. Unfortunately, the outside world was getting worse. In Ulm, political dissenters, free-thinkers, Jews, and other "enemies of the Reich" began disappearing into the void of the Fort Oberer Kuhberg concentration camp in the nearby hills. In 1941, the Scholls attended a sermon by Clemens August Graf von Galen, Bishop of Munster, regarding the Nazis' euthanasia policy and persecution of the Catholic Church. The bishop was an outspoken critic of the Nazi regime: "Justice is the only solid foundation of any state," he said. "The right to life, to inviolability, to freedom is an indispensable part of any moral order of society."

Justice was in short order, however, in Nazi Germany. Hans and Sophie were so deeply affected by the bishop's words that they determined to print and publish the speech. It was the first revolutionary act of a group that would later publish many more pamphlets and would become known as the White Rose.

The White Rose Goes to Work

By 1942, Hans preceded Sophie and Inge in moving to Munich to attend university, and he already had a close circle of friends and confidants: Alexander Schmorell, a bright, energetic, imaginative fellow; Christoph Probst, an intellectual nature-lover; and Willi Graf, a brooding, contemplative young man. Hans had continued to attentively follow the tumultuous, bewildering political waves sweeping over his country in the midst of war, and Sophie looked forward to discussing the troubling state of affairs with her brother and his impassioned young friends. At first, Sophie did not realize that her brother had sought to continue his underground publishing venture, but when she found out, she predictably supported him and joined his resistance of the Nazi evil. Her realization came about six weeks after classes began, when the circulation of leaflets articulating the anti-regime position electrified the campus:

> Nothing is so unworthy of a civilized people as allowing itself to be governed without opposition by an irresponsible clique that has yielded to base instinct . . . It is certain that today every honest German is ashamed of his government. Who among us has any conception of the dimensions of shame that will befall us and our children when one day the veil has fallen from our eyes and the most horrible of crimes—crimes that infinitely outdistance every human measure—reach the light of day?

The anonymous author of the pamphlet urged resistance—a brazenly treasonous piece of advice. Also buried in this first major pamphlet of the White Rose was an unfortunately prescient observation: "Only a few recognized the threat of ruin, and the reward for their heroic warning was death."

Sophie was both elated and frightened when she recognized

her brother's words in the pamphlet. The selfless sacrifice she had applauded when the pamphlet's author was anonymous took on a more sinister significance when she realized the person placing himself in opposition to Hitler and within the sights of the Nazis' violent enforcers, the SS, was her own brother. Still, she agreed wholeheartedly with his sentiments and decided that if Hans insisted on this course of action, it would be better if she went along with him in his venture. As a member of the White Rose, Sophie learned the identities of the other members—Hans's friends Alex, Christoph, and Willi, as well as Kurt Huber, a philosophy professor at the university.

For the next nine months, the White Rose worked diligently to craft and distribute leaflets discussing the Nazi threat and urging passive resistance. Since in Hitler's Germany inciting resistance to the Nazi regime was a capital crime and due process was expendable, the members of the group had to completely trust each other. Each time a new pamphlet was completed, the students secretively toted them to the school and left them in hallways and classrooms, where other students picked them up and soaked in messages laden with quotes from Goethe, Schiller, Aristotle, and other thinkers whose literature had been banned since the Nazis took power. At each moment, members of the White Rose knew they were risking their lives, for the words of their first pamphlet were magnified with each new publication. They knew the Nazi reward for such heroism was death.

On February 18, 1943, Sophie and Hans, laden with suitcases carrying their sixth pamphlet, arrived on campus. Messages written in tar, "Down with Hitler" and "Freedom"—the handiwork of Hans and Alex—still marred various walls around the campus. The brother and sister excitedly stacked pamphlets in high-traffic areas around the school. Then, after depositing them at all their previous locations, they realized they had some left over. In an act of desperate, dramatic defiance, they climbed to the top floor and flung the leaflets down to the corridors below. But their elation at their act of subversion evaporated when a voice beneath them shouted, "You're under arrest!"

The building's custodian, Jakob Schmid, had witnessed the unconventional delivery of the pamphlets and was determined to distinguish himself by catching the notorious scofflaws. As Sophie and Hans tried to escape, the building's doors were locked, and Schmid caught up with the pair and restrained them.

SS investigators arrived shortly. Initially they were skeptical that the two apparently straight-A students were responsible for blanketing the school in treasonous literature. Prolonged interrogation, however, eventually wore down the brother-sister team, and each confessed to a litany of severe crimes. To their credit, each tried to claim full responsibility for the actions of the White Rose, but the SS was a sophisticated, wide-reaching organization and several members of the group were soon imprisoned. Hans, Sophie, Christoph, Alex, Kurt, and Willi faced not only trial but the most severe potential punishment: execution.

Injustice in the Palace of Justice

Only days later, prison guards led Christoph, Hans, and Sophie to the Palace of Justice, the home of the People's Court—a building that had one of the most inappropriate names in history, for it hosted some of the most unjust trials ever conducted. The presiding judge, Roland Friesler, had been president of the court since mid-1942, and he was one of the most evil, opportunistic, and thoroughly objectionable people in the Third Reich. Friesler had been a devoted Bolshevik in the years after the first World War, but by 1925 he had flipped and become a committed National Socialist. He greatly admired Andrei Vishinsky, the prosecutor general of the USSR, who had carried out Stalin's Great Purge a few years earlier. Vishinsky was notorious for his trial tactics, which consisted mostly of vituperative, hyperbolic tirades against usually defenseless courtroom opponents. His advocacy, according to a 1947 *Time* magazine cover story, consisted of "shouting monstrous falsifications as matters of legal fact."

In his role as president of the People's Court, Friesler abandoned any facade of neutrality and adopted Vishinsky's approach. When the trial began at 10:00 a.m., he was bedecked in scarlet robes as he called the court to order. Gestapo interrogators sat ready to give sanitized testimony on the defendants' confessions. The charges—high treason and aiding and abetting the enemy—were presented. Then Friesler began berating the defendants, opening a spigot of vitriol without allowing interruptions from attorneys for either party. As physical evidence, but almost as an afterthought, court officials offered the White Rose duplicating machine and its pamphlets.

At last, satisfied that he had had his say, Friesler allowed each defendant a brief statement. Hans and Sophie remained silent. In a plea that went unheeded, Christoph asked for clemency. All three were sentenced to death. And within three days all three had been guillotined.

A Broader Legacy in Jurisprudence

Although their capture, trial, and execution took only days, Hans, Sophie, and the other martyred members of the White Rose left an enduring legacy. Their final pamphlet was smuggled out of Germany, reprinted, and airdropped over German cities and the German countryside. Today, in and around Munich, the names of the brave dissidents identify streets, plazas, and fountains. Beyond the monuments, however, they have left a broader legacy in jurisprudence, policy, and an ongoing discussion of the role of judges in government.

After the war, during the Justice Trial in Nuremberg, sixteen jurists from the Reich Ministry of Justice, People's Court, and Special Court were tried for war crimes and crimes against humanity. Somewhat ironically, under international law, the People's Court judges were given a fair trial, overseen by judges from the United States of America, for perverting justice.

The dramatic courtroom discussions during the Justice Trial touched not only on factual matters about the particular defendants, but also on general matters of jurisprudence and the widespread miscarriage of justice in the German court system during the preceding two decades. It became evident that the government had dictated specific outcomes for nearly every trial, and had set down repugnant principles and procedures for entire classes of cases. In a letter to Friesler, Dr. Otto Georg Thierack, Reich Minister of Justice, had directed: "If a Jew—and a leading Jew at that—is charged with high treason—even if he is only an accomplice therein—he has behind him the hate and the will of Jewry to exterminate the German people. As a rule this will therefore be high treason and must be punished by the death penalty." And he had concluded, "In case you should ever be in doubt as to which line to follow or which political necessities to take into consideration, please address yourself to me in all confidence." The government had offered such perverted guidance not only for racial discrimination, but also in political matters.

Based on the mountains of evidence and hours upon hours of testimony, ten of the sixteen defendants were convicted. Friesler escaped courtroom justice only because he had already been meted a larger measure of justice: In 1945, while he was overseeing a trial, a bomb dropped by Allied aircraft had killed him.

Justice as the Whim of a Small Clique

In the courts of the Third Reich, justice—elsewhere usually considered to be based on moral or ethical absolutes—was rendered an entirely relative concept. It was considered capable of rapid change, even reversal, upon the whim of a small clique of ruling elite. Adjudicating cases, judges found no guiding principles to consult, no consistent rule of law to call upon. Rather, in any given case, they had to wait for the executive to determine the "rule" to be applied. If the danger of such a capricious, unstable method of adjudication was not previously evident, after the debacle of the People's Court there can be no doubt that executive orders have no place in the courts.

In the Third Reich, constant pressure on the judiciary to make decisions conform to political objectives eroded the judiciary until it became a mere administrative body without discretion—capable of the most grievous violations of human rights. If such ordinary citizens as Sophie and Hans were willing to risk their lives to challenge the injustice around them, certainly judges—those specifically entrusted with cultivating justice—might have made a stand against Hitler's regime of terrible injustice. Instead, just as Lord Pitmilly elevated his own political and pecuniary interests above those of the Highland settlers, the People's Court judges conformed their conduct to Hitler's will. Their specific motivation in abandoning their independent discretion is inconsequential. Out of fear, greed, opportunism, or indifference, it makes no difference—the result was wrongful imprisonment, torture, genocide, and one of the darkest chapters in human history.

4

Bench and Bar
in the People's Republic of China

*One of the most hazardous jobs one can have in China is
human rights lawyer. And it's getting worse, experts and
lawyers say. About 50 of the 143,000 lawyers in China
regularly take on cases in which people fight jail terms for
speaking their minds or practicing their faith, or sue the
government over corruption and malfeasance. Increasingly,
these lawyers find themselves being targeted along with their
clients by a Communist Party that directs all manner of
Chinese justice.*
—Calum MacLeod, *USA TODAY*, December 11, 2009

IN AUGUST 2008, IN THE OPENING CEREMONY FOR THE OLYMPIC
games, the captivated world watched the People's Republic of China
showcase centuries of art and cultural evolution with breathtaking
displays of choreography and intricate synchronization. There in
elated Beijing, massive scrolls unfolded, thousands of drummers
with glowing drumsticks held a perfect beat, and an armory of fire-
works exploded above thousands of international fans.

During the seven years between its selection as host country and
its resplendent opening ceremony, China undertook one of history's
most impressive and extensive urban-development campaigns. But
almost obscured in the flurry of construction and measures to abate

pollution was China's other promise to the International Olympic Committee—its commitment to abate violations of human rights in the society that many experts cite as the world's foremost violator of such rights. And the Amnesty International Report 2008 noted that, despite Beijing's assurances, human-rights violations in China actually worsened in the years leading up to the games. For instance, despite an official ruling by the Supreme People's Court that death penalty cases must be heard in open court, most capital punishment trials have remained closed to the public, international observers, and the media. Further, the accused are presumed guilty, are regularly refused counsel, and, to extract confessions, are commonly tortured by the police. Lawyers are not even allowed to meet with their clients without first asking the government for permission. It is frequently withheld.

Human-rights violations in China persist, in part, because of the relative weakness of the rule of law. While the law-making process in post-Mao China has improved, it is still an amorphous, highly politicized cauldron of conflicting interests and influences. The Chinese Communist Party (CCP), striving to project a unified, cohesive front, retains strong control over all aspects of the legislative and judicial processes. Judges are subjugated to the government and face intense pressure to make their decisions conform to CCP directives, and those who do not conform are promptly removed from their posts. They also face such harsh punishments as jail time and re-education through labor—a method of administrative detention that persists despite sporadic attempts to rid the country of the practice.

Innocent, Executed, Permanently Convicted

In March 1995, a young man, Nie Shubin, was arrested and accused of raping and murdering a woman in a local cornfield.

During a grueling, protracted police interrogation, he continued to profess his innocence. A month later, when Mr. Nie's father sought to visit his son in prison, he was heartbroken to learn that he had not only been convicted of the crime, but had already been executed. Within thirty days, Nie Shubin had been arrested, convicted, and shot to death.

Through their grief, his parents steadfastly held to their son's innocence. Over the next decade, they maintained a campaign to clear his name. He was already dead, true, but erasing the stigma would vindicate his memory and clear the family name. Nie Shubin would be left a tragic martyr—a better fate than to be remembered forever as a murderer.

Five years later, in March 2005, another man confessed to the crime, and it quickly became apparent that Nie Shubin's pleas of innocence were true. Nie's parents then hired a lawyer named Zhang Huanzi to clear their son's name. When Zhang petitioned the court for a posthumous appeal, however, it informed him that it would not consider an appeal until he supplied a copy of the judgment against Nie Shubin. That requirement presented a problem: Only the court itself had access to the records, and it refused to provide them to Zhang. He and Nie Shubin's parents were stuck in a government-constructed Catch-22. So, to this day, as far as the Chinese government is concerned, Nie Shubin—convicted and executed for a crime he did not commit—is still officially a rapist and murderer.

"I Would Prefer to Be a Judge"

Between 1997 and 2002, at least five hundred Chinese lawyers were detained for reasons directly related to their efforts to uphold the rule of law while representing defendants. A 2003 report of the United States Congressional-Executive Commission on China studied the troubling trend of arrest and intimidation of such defense attorneys. The commission concluded that the issue of lawyers becoming defendants "poses a major challenge to China's criminal justice system and the Chinese leadership's stated goals of building the rule of law and protecting the rights of People's Republic of China citizens."

While China has taken some positive steps toward modernizing its justice process and improving universal access to the legal system, economic progress consistently outpaces legal reform, and economic rights and legal duties still outweigh considerations of individual legal rights. Judges and lawyers continue to find themselves under attack for ignoring political considerations and seeking to secure or redeem individual rights. In 2003, Zheng Enchong, a lawyer who sued a prominent real-estate developer on behalf of a group of poor Shanghai residents, found himself in more trouble than his clients. He had sued the state-supported real-estate developer after more than five hundred families were displaced from their homes to make room for a pre-Olympic urban-development project. Upon demanding his clients' rights to fair compensation for their deprivation of property, he received a three-year prison sentence for allegedly violating the state secrets law—an edict that allows the government to avoid normal criminal procedure when it determines that an individual committed an act that risked national security or threatened the bubble of secrecy surrounding the CCP. The law never defines the outer limits of what constitutes a "state secret," so the government has applied it extraordinarily broadly, holding at various times that it encompasses statistics on the numbers of drug addicts, HIV-AIDS sufferers, executed prisoners, and unemployed individuals, as well as on poverty rates, environmental disasters, public health, and industrial accidents.

After his conviction for violating the state secrets law, Mr. Zheng hired a lawyer to appeal his sentence. His lawyer was then accused of an unnamed constitutional violation and was banned from practicing law for one year.

Chinese jurists have scant liberty to choose the trajectories of their careers, especially if they gain a reputation for rocking the political boat or, put another way, advocating the rule of law. In fact, China appears to be willing to bridle lawyers for any reason or no reason at all. One example is Thomas G. Guo, a Chinese human-rights lawyer who agreed to be interviewed for this book. The transcript of that conversation appears in the Appendix on page 125. It details his experience with the government and his transformation from would-be judge to exiled human-rights lawyer.

Guo began his career auspiciously, but he soon ran into trouble. In 1984, after graduating with a law degree from Jilin University, he was sent to Fujian province to be a judge in the provincial high court. Before he took his post, however, the government revoked his position and appointed a more favored party member. Guo was transferred to the Fujian Foreign Economic Law Firm. "I would prefer to be a professor or judge instead of a lawyer," he noted, but all his requests to reclaim his spot on the bench were refused because of his political views.

Three years later, Guo had his first confrontation with the government when his girlfriend found a letter he had written that was critical of the CCP's heavy hand. She turned it over to the government, and his political beliefs earned him a one-year suspension from the practice of law. From that point on, the situation only deteriorated. In 1995, while Guo was working as counsel for a Hong Kong business, the government threatened to suspend his license again if he did not comply with directives from the Justice Minister. The situation escalated, and in 1999 police officers in Fuzhou, the capital city of Fujian province, threatened Guo's life, precipitating a move to Shanghai.

After enduring police harassment in Hong Kong and hearing

from former classmates and colleagues who had had similar experiences, Guo made a bold decision. He decided to leave the relative safety of mainstream practice and focus instead on defending human-rights cases.

If Guo thought his career until then was fraught with danger, his new life as a human-rights lawyer would make him sentimental for the old days. For example, in the eighteen months after he began defending persecuted practitioners of Falun Gong—also known as Falun Dafa, a spiritual movement that incorporates both Buddhist and Taoist principles—and other government targets, he was visited thirty-one times by the secret police.

The CCP believed that Guo's relentless efforts on behalf of political prisoners and defendants was subversive. The harassment escalated. In 2005, Shanghai Justice Bureau agents—ten strong—stormed his office and confiscated his computer and client information. Following the raid, the Justice Bureau on the one hand scheduled an open hearing and on the other began arresting anyone who planned to attend it. At the hearing, the bureau gave Guo a choice: Surrender your license for a year or be permanently banned from practicing law in China. Two days later, thirty policemen charged into Guo's house, seized his journal and cell phone, and took him to the police station. Released on bail, he was placed under house arrest for two months.

Mr. Guo had had enough. Without friends or funds but with luck, he found his way to Vancouver, British Columbia, where I interviewed him over the phone. Harassment, he said, has not stopped, and he has watched nervously as the secret police tap his phone, listen to his calls home, and surveil his family around the clock.

Mr. Guo pointed out that his experience, along with those of Messrs. Nie, Zhang, and Zheng, shows the dangers of the ancient Confucian Li-Fa System, which applies to everyone. The system dictates carefully graded relationships but is muddled in contemporary China.

As Thomas Guo also commented, he and the other Chinese dissidents who have fought the system must deal with the judiciary in China. He points out that the judges who hold long tenure are those who are politically sensitive, not those who make sound decisions based on the law. While Article 19 of the People's Republic of China Judges Law purports to base the advancement of judges on such factors as performance, professionalism, and ethics, in reality it is based more on the ability of judges to gain the trust of the CCP—and that trust is not earned by sound, consistent rulings, but rather by deference to the government's position. Guo makes the keen observation that the Judges Law shows the extent of judicial disembowelment. It speaks, he says, not of judges' power to exercise trial and adjudicate, but rather of the court's power. While those two concepts are usually synonymous, the CCP uses the latent ambiguity to justify shackling judges to the will of the party.

Practice Diverges from Theory

In Vancouver, where he himself at least is safe from reprisal, Mr. Guo pointed out that the practice of selecting judges diverges greatly from the theory and law purportedly governing the bench in China. According to Article 12 of the Judges Law, persons who meet standards of both ability and political integrity and who are to be appointed judges or assistant judges for the first time shall be selected, through public examination and strict appraisal, from among the best qualified for the posts.

Guo suggested that, in reality, until the beginning of the twenty-first century most of the bench was unqualified and had no legal education and possibly no higher education at all. He added that since judges were rarely required to exercise any sort of legal reasoning or knowledge of laws or procedures, there was no need for formal education. In fact, when seeking a job in the PRC's courts, knowledge was more of a liability than an asset. The lack of formal education created a lack of any adherence to legal norms, leading to vastly divergent results and practices in various provinces of the nation. Contradictory results arose from essentially similar controversies, and appeals were granted in some provinces while they were not available in others.

In the United States, all respectable law schools incorporate ethical training, or "Professional Responsibility" into their curricula, and passing a standardized PR exam is a prerequisite to sitting for the bar exam in almost every state. In China until very recently, since judges were not even required to attend law school, no such procedure existed. Predictably, judicial malfeasance became a common complaint and hushed stories circulated concerning judges blackmailing litigants, fabricating rulings, embezzling court funding, and asking outright for bribes in exchange for hearings or appeals.

Massive Corruption Scandal

While tales of corruption and injustice steadily undermined public confidence in the Chinese judiciary, the true extent of the problem was not clear until 2001, when a massive corruption scandal was publicized in Hubei province.

In Wuhan, the capital of the province, a disgruntled citizen complained that his "gift" to a criminal court judge had not led, as promised, to a review of his life sentence. Officials launched an investigation that lasted several years. It revealed startlingly pervasive corruption in Wuhan. When the dust settled, the party had disciplined almost eight hundred judges for irregularities, investigated fifty-two more for criminal offenses, and given lengthy prison sentences to thirteen judges, including two vice presidents of the Wuhan Inter-mediate People's Court. The judges profited over four million yuan ($500,000) from such activities as taking bribes from both plain-tiffs and defendants, manufacturing court cases and verdicts, selling evidence, and embezzling court funding. Government officials were embarrassed and, to their credit, vowed to fix the broken system.

With reforms still forthcoming, progress has been hampered by many of the same barriers that have plagued the system for years. A stable rule of law—the foundation of any effective legal system—has not materialized. Political interests regularly trump laws that appear to be flexible. And judges have yet to see any increase in discretion or improvement in independence on the part of those interested in political government.

Although the post-scandal study ignored the most obvious and important reforms, it did produce some incremental improvements. The investigation faulted the dominant Chinese appeal mecha-nism—the so-called "two-instance final adjudication system"—for creating strong incentives for parties to bribe judges to secure appel-late review. Under the system, after an initial decision most litigants are permitted just one appeal. While there are additional levels of appellate courts beyond the Intermediate People's Court, includ-ing the Higher People's Court and Supreme People's Court, cases rarely rise above one level of appellate review. Since opportunities for reversal are sparse, parties have tremendous incentives to bribe judges to secure appeals—and in doing so they have, essentially, nothing to lose.

The investigation also found that a method of rendering judg-ments called the "Collegiate Panel" created opportunities for brib-ery to flourish. In it, at least three judges preside together over a case and adjudicate it. In theory, such a judging panel renders opinions by consensus, but in reality the chief of the panel wields a disproportionately large share of power, so by bribing the chief judge one can defeat the safeguard that is supposed to be provided by a group decision.

In fact, legislation has for the first time, at least in the opinions of the Wuhan investigators, made legal education or experience a prerequisite to a judicial appointment. As a result, legal norms and ethical guidance have begun to trickle into the judicial system. But the old guard judges are still in power, along with a degree of political criticism, declining prospects for judicial careers, and even threats and imprisonment. Until the number of new, enlightened judges on the bench reaches a critical number where over-regulation and harassment can no longer be ignored—if the government allows that to happen—the climate is unlikely to improve significantly.

As Mr. Guo and others point out, the government, despite a lack of momentum, may be moving in the direction of constitutionalism. It expects—in fact, it requires—judges and lawyers to unquestioningly bend to government pressure. Political conformity is of paramount importance, and dire consequences follow for those who attempt to practice their profession according to the rule of law without regard for politics.

Late in 2009, *A Sword and a Shield: China's Human Rights Lawyers*, a book published by the China Human Rights Concern Group, drew attention to the plight of the nation's lawyers. The group's chairman, Albert Ho Chun-yan, said they "raise a sword to a system which is rotten to the root, and the government chooses to oppress them. The situation is getting worse, but this also shows they have a growing influence. They cause an impact on the system. They are the heroes of our time."

One expert on China's legal profession, associate professor Ethan Michelson of Indiana University, says the most outspoken of the country's rights lawyers "are on the lunatic fringe, almost guaranteed to get arrested or detained. I don't know why anyone would want to be a lawyer in China."

5

Destabilized Pakistan's Independent Judiciary

The situation in Pakistan has much to add to the discussion of judicial independence and courageous judges. Obviously, Justices Siddiqui, Chaudhry, and the others who refused to dishonor the precepts set forth in the constitution are exemplary leaders—examples of bold, principled jurists who understand the importance of the rule of law and who fight for its survival. But more, the way Pakistan's lawyers came to fight the judge and lead the public highlights the legal profession's importance in the struggle against totalitarianism.

FOR JUDGES WHO HAD SO MUCH POTENTIAL WHEN THE REPUBLIC of Pakistan was first conceived in the 1940s, the 1970s and '80s were devastating. In rapid succession, events unfolded that eroded judges' independence and the rule of law. A 1979 constitutional amendment created one hundred military courts, and a companion law prevented non-military courts from hearing challenges to martial law or decisions of the military courts. In addition, in 1980 the separate Federal Shariat Court was established with the power to invalidate laws deemed repugnant to Islamic law. The judges who had originally been so powerful became mere administrators. The seed of the rule of law, planted at the birth of the nation, had never grown.

Each time an international crisis materialized, the government strengthened its hold on society and the judiciary and asserted broad emergency powers. As the nation roiled with internal and external chaos, the executive began finding "state necessity" everywhere and using emergency rule to control every aspect of daily life.

Still, as the new millennium approached, Pakistan appeared to be stabilizing and approaching some semblance of constitutional consistency. Although military and civilian governments had essentially split time in office—civilians occupying the office of the presidency for twenty-two years and the military for twenty-three years—the country's third constitution, adopted in 1973, was still operative. A bruised Pakistan had survived major skirmishes with India in 1965 and 1971 and then a civil war in 1975. Yet, despite the ongoing turmoil, the military had stayed out of the government since 1988, and independent-minded judges were gradually becoming optimistic that the rule of law might take root. They were sorely mistaken.

The New Crisis

On October 13, 1999, Prime Minister Nawaz Sharif sat in his office in the Secretariat in Islamabad. The critics had been riding him lately, accusing his administration of corruption in various aspects of government and of mishandling disputes and sectarian violence both in Kashmir and within the borders of Pakistan. He had also drawn both praise and disapproval for advocating a constitutional amendment to prevent the president from dismissing an elected prime minister. Still, it was his second term and he had endured criticism for years, so he was confident he would outlast the latest spate of bad press.

Sharif was more worried about the repercussions of his latest official action. He had good reason to worry, for he had just dismissed his powerful military chief, General Pervez Musharraf, and he knew that the military, having held the very highest office in the country numerous times in the past fifty years, clearly had an eye on many of the government's highest offices.

Only hours after he was dismissed, General Musharraf appeared on television announcing that the military was removing the prime minister from office. Thus, ten years after the last previous coup, and without a shot being fired, Sharif lost his position and the military was back in power. The public barely batted an eye.

In the middle of the night on October 15, now-President Musharraf issued a provisional constitutional order that barred the courts of Pakistan not only from challenging the constitutionality of any executive action but also from issuing any order against the president or anyone in his administration.

This provisional order made manifest what had been an unspoken policy for decades, for despite provisions in the 1956 and 1973 constitutions explicitly identifying the supreme court as the interpreter of the constitution, the executive had long considered itself above constitutional scrutiny. Confirming an unspoken custom, Musharraf made it official policy: The oath of office was subordinate to a judge's loyalty to the executive branch of government.

While Musharraf was laying the foundation for the evisceration of the judiciary, he repeatedly assured judges that they would not be affected by the change in regime. According to him, Sharif was the bad guy, and judges and the public should applaud the new president's efforts to free the judiciary from his grasp. Musharraf promised judges they would not be required to ignore their constitutional oaths and would face only minor tweaks in jurisdiction intended to improve the efficiency of the justice system.

Despite all of Musharraf's promises, however, the situation changed when deposed prime minister Sharif initiated legal action challenging the military takeover. Now, as the supreme court agreed to entertain a hearing on the legitimacy of the new government, Musharraf began to feel the heat from the spurned judiciary. The members of the bench, infuriated by his provisional constitutional order, appeared ready to strike back with a ruling favorable to Sharif.

Just as the court was about to issue their decision, Musharraf struck another blow to judicial independence. Using his emergency powers, he issued an "Oath of Office Order" that required judges to swear loyalty to him and his provisional constitutional order rather than to the 1973 constitution. The judges who refused the new oath were deemed unqualified to sit on the bench and were forced out of their offices. They were replaced with Musharraf-loyalists who would support the general and conform the law to his standards.

Pakistan's Judges Fight Back

In 1954 and 1955, the Assembly of Pakistan, trying to establish checks on the powers of Governor General Ghulam Muhammad, had moved to change the constitution, but Muhammad had thwarted the assembly by using his reserve powers to dismiss it—an action the supreme court upheld. Following that, judges had mostly remained passive and accepted downgrading to positions as executive sidekicks. For some, the government's justification may have proved compelling: Pakistan had been roiling with turmoil throughout most of its history, so some may have seen a need for a strong executive with extensive emergency powers. For others, the dangers of challenging the extra-constitutional government probably provided sufficient motivation to stay quiet.

When Musharraf suspended the constitution and broke his promise to the judiciary by requiring them to ignore their constitutional oath, he found he had overestimated the judges' passivity— and Pakistan found the trajectory of its struggle with the rule of law on a new course. The president's duplicity infuriated Chief Justice

Saiduzzaman Siddiqui, who refused to swear loyalty to Musharraf. Five other supreme court justices, two judges of the Lahore High Court, three judges of the High Court of Sindh, and two judges of the Peshawar High Court followed his lead. All lost their seats on the bench, and Chief Justice Siddiqui was placed under house arrest. The remaining judges who had pledged their loyalty to Musharraf, along with their new colleagues, the loyalist replacements for the uncooperative judges, predictably upheld Musharraf's coup. Although the five courageous supreme court justices were no longer in a position to directly resist the executive encroachment into the judiciary, in the public's eyes they became the first heroes of the cause—a development that would prove to be more powerful than anyone hoped.

Musharraf won the election in 2002, but he faced accusations that the election by referendum had been rigged to achieve results favoring him. Undeterred, he sought and secured a vote of confidence from Parliament that allowed him to retain his post as commander of the armed forces as well as president. Empowered by the two victories, he continued to push the limits of his power and to test the resolve of the judiciary. In 2003, he signed the Legal Framework Order, which gave him the power to dismiss the prime minister, dissolve the national assembly, and appoint army commanders and regional governors.

As the new election approached in 2007, Musharraf sensed he was becoming unpopular and was at risk of losing the presidency. He made his first mistake in March. After unsuccessfully trying to get supreme court justice Iftikhar Chaudhry to tender his resignation, Musharraf dismissed him on charges of misconduct. (Chaudhry had actually drawn criticism in the past for being too pro-government. In 2000, for example, as a supreme court justice, he had helped legitimize Musharraf's initial declaration of martial law, and in 2002 he had helped the general keep his military position while also serving as president. After his elevation to chief justice in 2005, however, Chaudhry had begun distancing himself from the president. By the time of the 2007 election, Chaudhry and Musharraf were no longer allied, and many suspected that if Musharraf triumphed Chaudhry would launch a review of the election.)

Support for the Troublesome Judge

Musharraf won re-election and had apparently been able to re-move Justice Chaudhry. Other judges had earlier tried to question his authority and he had removed them, keeping them quiet with threats and intimidation while he went about the business of rul-ing the country. This time, he assumed, would be no different, but he had underestimated this chief justice, and his mistake would cost him dearly. Immediately after his termination, Chaudhry an-nounced that he would not fade away quietly but would embark on a cross-country tour, speaking out against Musharraf in regional bar associations and public forums.

Everywhere Chaudhry went, thousands of people came out to support the rare public show of criticism against the regime. They greeted him as a hero. The establishment, however, saw him as a revolutionary. In an effort to scare away would-be support-ers, Musharraf sent troops to Chaudhry's rallies, and violence was common wherever he spoke. A few weeks into his journey, when he tried to enter Karachi to address the Sindh High Court Bar As-sociation, a riot erupted as activists from the Musharraf-friendly Muttahida Quami Movement tried to disperse Chaudhry support-ers. Hundreds were injured, and forty-two people lost their lives.

Not only did Chaudhry have popular support, but the supreme court also sided with him. In July, it found no cause for his dismissal and reinstated him to his position as chief justice. This setback, along with the court's show of independence, infuriated Musharraf.

He was further incensed when a retired supreme court justice and opposition candidate in the recent election, Wajhuddin Ahmed, disputed the election results. Ahmed argued that a person holding the office of chief of army staff was not constitutionally permitted to run for president, yet Musharraf had been holding both titles for five years. The supreme court agreed to take the case.

Before the supreme court could render a decision on Ahmed's challenge, Musharraf formally declared a state of emergency and, for the second time in his presidency, suspended the constitution. To rein in the "rogue" judiciary, he issued another provisional constitutional order and vowed to dismiss any judge who did not swear an oath to it. This had worked the first time in 1999, when Siddiqui's dissidence was contained by the revised oath and a stint under house arrest. But this time was different. Encouraged by the independent stance of Chief Justice Chaudhry, a full two-thirds of the country's senior judges refused to take the oath. Chaudhry also launched a supreme court review of Musharraf's state of emergency, and, while nothing like this had ever happened in the brief history of Pakistan, the chief justice continued to gain public support.

In an act of desperation, Musharraf sent an army brigade to the supreme court to arrest Chaudhry and the other judges who refused to take the oath. To prevent them from organizing resistance, he put them under house arrest and replaced them with a puppet court of political allies. Although he achieved his desired result from the new court of loyalists, who promptly dismissed Ahmed's election challenge, Musharraf was in trouble. The nation did not stand idly by. To show they had finally tired of Musharraf's constitutional manipulations, judges and lawyers gathered and launched one of the most extensive political movements in the country's history, taking to the streets and boycotting courts across the nation. The justice system was paralyzed.

Although Musharraf tried again to use the military and police forces to solve the enormous public relations crisis, he had lost public support. The public backed the courageous chief justice in his fight for independence from the overreaching executive. Indeed, embattled judges and downtrodden lawyers made more sympathetic figures than the rampaging president and his army. And each time demonstrating jurists and police clashed, newspapers decried the heavy-handed, often violent tactics of those in uniform.

Musharraf Loses Control

Moreover, the suspension of the constitution compromised international support. Since 2001, the United States had cautiously backed Musharraf because he promised to continue aiding the American war on terror. His suspension of the constitution, however, destabilized Pakistan and diverted resources from fighting terrorism to maintaining law and order. Only five days after Musharraf's declaration of a state of emergency, while the military was busy trying to stifle public demonstrations by lawyers and judges, Islamic militants took over the city of Madyan, a popular tourist destination in the northwest corner of the country. A month later, after a political rally leading up to parliamentary elections, a former prime minister and popular opposition candidate, Benazir Bhutto, was assassinated. Musharraf appeared to be losing control of Pakistan. His popularity—already hurting from his public battle with the judiciary—began a sustained decline.

The tumult continued during the winter months. During police crackdowns on public rallies, scores of lawyers dedicated to an independent judiciary were wounded. Many lost their jobs and others were imprisoned. In March 2008, four months after Musharraf's second suspension of the constitution, the movement gained its first victory as newly elected prime minister Syed Yousuf Raza Gilani announced his support for freeing imprisoned judges, including

Iftikhar Chaudhry. Although in Pakistan the prime minister does not outrank the president, his position carries some weight because he is elected by the dominant coalition in Parliament. Gilani's announcement gave the embattled judges hope and kindled speculation that the reeling Musharraf would soon be out of office.

They were right. After months of public demonstrations and heated arguments between coalitions in Parliament, it became clear that Musharraf could not maintain order in the country. By June 2008, he was crippled, and by August he was forced to resign. After a military coup, nine years in office, two states of emergency, two provisional constitutions, and skirmishes with Islamic militants and India, it was a few thousand jurists and members of the bar dedicated to the rule of law who brought Musharraf down.

Unfortunately the story does not end there. History has taught, and Pakistan bears it out, that political parties support judicial independence as long as their interests are the same, but as soon as their interests diverge, they decry judges as activists overreaching their power. Even Musharraf was a supporter of Iftikhar Chaudhry early in Chaudhry's administration, when he was making favorable rulings. But as soon as the court's rulings against the regime began to come down, Chaudhry was an enemy. Likewise, the administration of Pakistan President Asif Ali Zardari enthusiastically supported Chaudhry's campaign for judicial independence while it was helping their candidate's popularity, but that support faded after Zardari realized that restoring Chaudhry to the bench would give the chief justice oversight over the new administration. A year after his dismissal and six months after the Zardari administration took power, Chaudhry was still waiting to get his job back, proving that one test of whether the executive sincerely supports judicial independence is whether or not support continues after the court hands down rulings unfavorable to the administration.

Paradoxically, hope for the rule of law in Pakistan lies in the fact that Pakistani judges are managing to offend every political party and continually find themselves in the unenviable position of government pariahs. The judges garnering the most criticism are often the ones who refuse to play political games and insist on following the rule of law in their courtrooms. If they went along with the interests of the ruling political party, they would undoubtedly have much easier lives and longer careers—but as long as they continue to respect the rule of law in the face of heavy-handed, uncompromising regimes, they will need to remain strong and act courageously.

With the support of lawyers and the public, the judges' movement in Pakistan has continued to fight, while the government has pledged support but covertly obstructed its progress. Daily gaining momentum, the movement has shown that it has the capability to effect significant change. Let us hope the rule of law has taken root. As long as courageous judges and lawyers continue speaking out, it has a chance to grow and blossom.

6

A Serbian Judge Fights for the Rule of Law

On July 19, 2002, a small woman with reddish hair streaked with gray stepped onto an awards platform in Moscow. She stood quietly as an attorney from Washington read aloud a litany of her accomplishments—from raising the wages of the Serbian judiciary to founding the first Serbian Judicial Association. Her usually serious countenance broke into a broad smile as, accompanied by deafening applause from her fellow international jurists, she became the inaugural recipient of the American Bar Association Central European and Eurasian Law Initiative Reformer's Award (a title changed in later years to the ABA Rule of Law Initiative Reformer's Award). The event was one of the few public acknowledgments of her work. Her home country, Serbia, like other countries where the rule of law is honored in the breach, has mostly ignored her story or actively prevented it from being told.

SERBIA IS A FORMER STATE OF THE YUGOSLAV FEDERATION, WHICH was dissolved by the bloody wars in the 1990s in the Balkans. In that decade, the regime was headed by Slobodan Milosevic, a notoriously repressive leader. From 1991 to 1995, he ordered hundreds of thousands of non-Serbs to be forcibly expelled from their homes. Thousands more were killed, assaulted, or imprisoned in brutal and degrading facilities in municipalities across Croatia, Bosnia, Herzegovina, Serbia, and Montenegro. These were some of the most serious violations of human rights in Europe since World War II. Ultimately, on charges of crimes against humanity, Milosevic was brought to the International Criminal Tribunal for the former Yugoslavia at the Hague in the Netherlands, a body authorized in 1993 by the United Nations Security Council. He died there in detention in March 2006.

Milosevic ascended to power in 1988, eight years after the death of Josip Broz, commonly known as Marshall Tito, who had united Bosnia, Herzegovina, Croatia, the Republic of Macedonia, Montenegro, Serbia, and Slovenia into the Socialist Federal Republic of Yugoslavia. Led by Tito, Serbia had developed a functioning court system that demonstrated a semblance of the rule of law. While not entirely free from political influence, the country's judges were respected, and those who studied law had to undergo special training before coming to the bench. Judges themselves were by and large independently minded, knowing that if they performed their duties well they would be promoted, over time, to increasingly prominent positions within the judiciary. The public also generally thought of the judiciary as competent, impartial, and operating without significant interference.

When Slobodan Milosevic was elected president of Serbia in 1988, competing powers were struggling for political domination. His party promised unification. Once in control, however, he began to dismantle structures that could threaten his centralization of power. This attempt focused not only on ethnic and political groups, but also on such independent institutions as the judiciary. It was in this transitioning climate that Judge Leposava Karamarkovic came to the bench.

Interview in Belgrade

In 1991, Judge Karamarkovic was appointed to the supreme court of Serbia. For nearly a decade, with a backdrop of war, repression, and genocide under the brutal regime of Slobodan Milosevic, she fought for the rule of law and the independence of judges.

While doing research for this book, I went to Belgrade, where Judge Karamarkovic sat until 2003 and where, by the time of my interview, she had become a professor of law at the University of Belgrade. Her nephew, who worked at the time for the American Bar Association, met my wife and me at the airport and took us to her office. Most importantly, he spoke English. We recorded the interview, and of course the excerpts reproduced in this chapter are his translations into English.

Judge Karamarkovic described the two ways in which Milosevic started his attack on the judiciary. First, favored politicos were made judges, sometimes with no formal legal training. Appointed judges who were obedient to Milosevic and his goals were promoted, while independent judges remained sidelined in the lower courts. When asked how responsive judges were to political manipulation, Judge Karamarkovic answered:

Members of the judiciary always had a feeling that they had to obey. This is not something that Milosevic introduced. He just enlarged on it. The members of the judiciary were never loud, you know, with their statements, but Milosevic found a way to manipulate the fact that the judges were never loud in their opinions. Before Milosevic, members of the judiciary . . . were professional. . . . [After Milosevic] there was really no profession anymore. People were starting to join parties in order to be able to have a profession or become a judge. That's why everyone was quiet and it was not wise to be loud to the supreme court. Honest judges started to leave. You saw cases where in a very short time a municipal judge would become a supreme court judge, sometimes not even coming out of the judiciary, just be appointed.

These changes happened subtly, and most judges did not immediately see how the institution was being politically manipulated.

The second form of interference was more insidious. Judge Karamarkovic described how court presidents, who were responsible for case assignments, were instructed that politically sensitive cases were to go to judges willing to rule in line with the government. This approach, which made it apparent that government-favored defendants received particularly light punishments or were allowed to go free, resulted in a further disintegration of the rule of law. To ensure this conduct would continue and to reward jurists who followed the party line, certain judges were given ". . . condos, apartments, good credit ratings and they began to climb up the ladder, advancing in the system." These political favors were particularly effective in light of stagnant judicial salaries and rapid inflation. The judge put it this way:

> Before hyperinflation the salaries of members of the judiciary were quite good actually, and then everything crashed like a tower of cards and all members of society, completely, independently, had very low wages, like five or six Deutsche marks per month. And in that particular crisis, 1992, 1993, 1994, the system found a way to influence certain judges. I mean if a certain judge doesn't have a wage it's easy to have a big influence. Nominally they get the same salary like last month, but last month you could have bought let's say . . . a jacket and now you can buy a bottle of beer for the same amount of money.

Many judges felt that the precariousness of their livelihoods contributed to the rise in judicial corruption. No mechanism was available for independent judges to challenge attempts by the government to influence case proceedings. To address these problems,

Judge Karamarkovic and others decided that the judges needed a voice, and she spearheaded the formation of the first Judges Association. Judge Karamarkovic described its founding:

> A core represented by the two of us from the supreme court and the judges from the constitutional court and several from the municipal and from district courts [in total about 15]. . . . We were trying to activate the other members of the judiciary and to provoke them into some kind of action against what was going on. These were the best of the best of the best in the judiciary, and first of all independent, very important. The reason [for the association's formation] . . . was in part due to our awareness that three to five obedient judges were seen to find good reasons to let the guilty go free. They would say the evidence was not properly admitted and find procedural and bureaucratic reasons to let criminals go free. We would make a statement about it, we would speak out.

During the turbulent times of the 1990s, the Judges Association spoke out against the government's illegal activities, identifying corruption as it occurred and demanding increases in judicial salaries. At its height, the association included some five hundred members whose newfound sense of independence soon drew Milosevic's ire, and judges started finding themselves dismissed. Judge Karamarkovic described how the reprisals began after the government was sent an open letter:

> The real repression started when five of us—I was the only woman, there were four other men from the supreme court— wrote an open letter . . . [that] openly said the elections were stolen. We pointed our fingers at the judges who were involved in . . . the election process. . . . I was a Supreme Court judge

with respect in the community and when a judge was dismissed overnight I signed my name, as all the judges in the association did, to let the community know the kind of repression Milosevic had brought to Serbia and how the rule of law was being [dishonored].

By 1997, Serbia was in utter turmoil. For 119 days straight, primarily to pressure the government into recognizing local election results, University of Belgrade students held protests.

The Judges Association also had to go underground, as the government refused to recognize us on the grounds that "goals of the association [were deemed] opposite to the goals of the state." As a consequence, there was incessant government dismissals of judges. Court presidents would in organizing court sessions require each judge to announce publicly whether he or she was a member of the Judges Association. Such reprisals resulted in approximately two thousand judges being fired.

As a cofounder of the Judges Association, Judge Karamarkovic could not escape this fate, despite the fact that her position on the supreme court gave her life tenure. In March 2000, she was dismissed from the bench. She recalls that she came to work and found on her desk a letter stating that she was no longer a judge. The letter had been signed by the president of the supreme court, who was "100 percent obedient to the regime."

I expected it, to be fair, and I expected it much earlier. They kept asking us, they kept asking me to stop, and I kept telling them that I'm doing this out of pure conviction and that as long as I firmly believe that this kind of activity this corruption of the courts was ongoing I planned to make my position clear and to speak out. And they would tell me—whoever was going—they will dismiss you, and I would say, well, so be it.

Not a single judge of the supreme court would say a word. No one protected us.

During the four years of our battle, no one would come to my office at the supreme court. I was never removed from the position of the president of the panel, but people were so afraid that no one would have communication with me.

Judge Karamarkovic explained that she believed that she was dismissed because of her role in getting a corrupt judge removed from the court. The case that brought this corruption to light involved the arrest of a state security agent. The agent was detained without access to his counsel or family, and his trial was fixed. Judge Karamarkovic described the role of the judge in the case:

The judge who was assigned . . . told us that before he was given this case, he had a meeting with the president of the court, a representative of the Ministry of Interior Affairs, and that they made a deal that this guy who was arrested would get two years' imprisonment. That was going to be the outcome of the trial. Since this was the first instance court, there were two lay judges [on] the panel. There was no proof, no evidence, there was only one notebook that was filled with his writing, handwriting. They pronounced this to be in violation of the official secrets law.

And when they concluded the trial and where there was a time, you know, the deliberation, and he proposed, you know, two years of imprisonment because he was the president of the panel. The lay judges said no, no, this man is not guilty. He was very scared by what the lay judges said and he just didn't know how to react and what to do. He just took the case . . . file . . . and took it to the people that had come to talk to him before the trial. He said there was nothing he could do, I couldn't get you the verdict that you wanted. They just changed the lay judges, they changed the president of the panel, so it was an entirely new panel, and this person was convicted and sentenced to spend two years in prison. We found out about this case [from] the lay judges. We had no way of finding out about all of the cases. . . .

In the end we managed to dismiss this judge, but it was very, very hard. It wasn't easy to do.

The Bulldozer Revolution Ends the Regime

In September 2000, the Democratic Opposition of Serbia (DOS), a coalition of parties opposed to the Milosevic regime, won a majority in the nationwide parliamentary election. The government refused to certify the results, leading to a protest spearheaded by a student group called *Otpor!*—or "Resistance!"

The protest started when coal miners in the Kolubara River region went on strike. It reached its height on October 5 as several hundred thousand protestors from all over Serbia arrived in Belgrade to march against the government. Unlike previous protests, there was no large-scale police crackdown, even though the protestors partially burned the Parliament building. When a bulldozer operator, Ljubisav Dokic, fired up his engine and used it to charge the Serbian Broadcasting Corporation building (called "RTS"), which for a decade had been a symbol of Milosevic's rule, the protest gained a permanent nickname: the Bulldozer Revolution. With the RTS studios taken over, the station was quickly renamed *Novi RTS* ("New RTS") as a sign that the regime had lost power. Milosevic resigned on October 7.

Vojislav Kostunica succeeded Milosevic as president of the Federal Republic of Yugoslavia and then became the Serbian prime minister. Trained in the law, Kostunica was a populist politician who was supported by both the "democratic" and "nationalistic" voters. He had no connection to the old communist party, from which Milosevic's party originated.

Upon Kostunica's rise to power, many felt that Serbia would at last make the transition to a democratic state. After the first parliamentary session under his presidency, all the judges who had been dismissed were reinstated, but with his great promises came great disappointments. Judge Karamarkovic recalled:

> After the year 2000, we had great expectations. We expected to be all on the same side, and we . . . expected them to respect the independence of the judiciary and to let us do our own thing. On the other hand, they expected us to respect them in a way that would let them do what they wanted.
>
> When coming to their new positions, they were involved in drafting the systematic law on the judiciary that would secure the independence of judges, prosecutors, etc. . . . when judges started to practice the guarantees given to the judiciary by the law the government amended those laws and took away the independence. . . .

Judge Karamarkovic explained. The crackdown on the judiciary, she said, resulted from the new government's insistence that its reforms happen overnight and in accordance with their agenda, rather than in a more orderly fashion and according to the rule of law.

> The judiciary insisted that while the transition was taking place the forms . . . happen in accordance with the law. The government saw us as a body . . . slowing them down. In Serbia's system [under Milosevic], you had professional judges and magistrates. Magistrates dealt with misdemeanors. By

using magistrates, [the government could impose] enormous fines [on the media] and actually shut them down in a way.

After the new government of the fifth of October came into power, they decided that those Magistrates who punished [the] independent media should be fired without resort to any procedural safeguards [at] trial. But the judiciary said no, we cannot do that, we have to follow the law before they can be dismissed; they must have a hearing.

This was a major obstacle that members of the judiciary, with Judge Karamarkovic in the forefront, insisted upon, while the government's position, as always, was: We just have to take them out of the picture.

"Best Professionals" Leave Office

In 2003, the assassination of Prime Minister Zoran Djindjic brought the tensions between the judiciary and the new government to a head. Djindjic, a philosophy professor, had been instrumental in bringing about Milosevic's downfall, and during his tenure the international community had hailed him as a true market reformer. Many believed that organized crime lords orchestrated his assassination.

The government used the crime as a method of tainting its opposition. When it even tried to implicate the judiciary in the assassination, said Judge Karamarkovic, she once again added her voice in opposition. Then, faced with almost sure dismissal, she decided to step down.

So you have a clear picture of how we left the court in 2003, I will tell you. I left, the prosecutors left, and all of the people of integrity and the best professionals from the supreme court also left at that time, in 2003 after the prime minister was assassinated, and immediately thereafter a state of emergency was declared. Completely anonymous people came from different cities, from Novi Sad, from elsewhere, came and filled out positions. . . . It was a state of emergency, and these were the people who were supposed to be fighting crime, criminal organized groups at the time, and to discover and convict the murderers of the prime minister.

In her interview with me, Judge Karamarkovic voiced her deep disappointment with the new regime, saying, "Yes, I was completely disappointed in 2003 because this was what we had fought for and we did everything we could to reignite the rule of law but without success."

Among post-communist and post-autocratic nations, Serbia's story is not unique. Judge Karamarkovic's courageous fight brought down one corrupt regime, but tensions arose between the instillation and adherence to new institutional principles such as the rule of law. Her hope is that her students will continue the struggle toward a new and democratic Serbia—one that recognizes and respects the role of an independent judiciary.

7

U.S. v. Bayless—*A Home-Grown Challenge to the Rule of Law*

In 1994, I was nominated and confirmed by the U.S. Senate for a seat on the busy United States District Court for the Southern District of New York. It sits in downtown Manhattan and is the destination of many of the most important commercial and criminal cases in the country. To be a member of that court was a dream I had harbored ever since I first went to work in 1961 as a young Assistant United States Attorney in the office of Robert M. Morgenthau.

Less than a year after I was confirmed, an event took place in Manhattan's Washington Heights that forever changed my thinking about America and prompted me to write this book. To an extent it changed the thinking of many Americans with respect to one of the pillars of our democracy—the rule of law.

—H.B., Jr.

THE WASHINGTON HEIGHTS AREA AT THE NORTHERN END OF Manhattan took its name from a hard-fought and agonizing defeat suffered by George Washington's young army during the American Revolution. While it has an illustrious past, that part of New York City became a neighborhood of violence and turmoil in the second half of the twentieth century. In 1965, civil rights activist

Malcolm X was assassinated while giving a speech in its Audubon Ballroom. Later, in the 1980s, a crack epidemic hit Washington Heights particularly hard as its poor, mostly immigrant population eagerly bought into the cheap narcotic highs that gave them brief respites from their despair.

The neighborhood continued to deteriorate, and violent crime exploded. Drug gangs based their operations there. In October 1988, a Dominican drug dealer shot and killed a young New York Police Department (NYPD) officer as he and his partner tried to arrest two suspects on drug charges. Marking the beginning of a truly destructive relationship between the police and the residents of Washington Heights, the officer's death called attention to the breadth of the violence plaguing the area, and the police, who in the past had been welcomed by the neighborhood's many upstanding residents, adopted more aggressive tactics to address the drug-gang problem.

An Investigation into Allegations of Police Corruption

At this time—1992, to be precise—I had just resigned as a justice of the New York State Supreme Court and was appointed as one of the five unpaid members of a new commission created by Mayor David Dinkins to investigate police corruption. The commission soon took on the name of its chairman, Milton Mollen, a former presiding justice of the Appellate Court and more recently a deputy mayor. Because I had previously served as the Chief of the Organized Crime and Racketeering Unit in the United States Attorney's Office for the Southern District of New York and later as the First Assistant United States Attorney and Chief of the Criminal Division in that office, it was considered that my experience might be helpful to the commission. Our mission was to find out if the rampant allegations of police corruption were true.

New York City has a long history of commissions to investigate corruption in its police department. Beginning as far back as the New York State Senate's Lexow Committee in 1894 and concluding with Mayor John V. Lindsay's Knapp Commission, which was created in April 1970, a new one has been formed just about every twenty years. A major allegation that undoubtedly helped convince the mayor to form the commission was that the police not only were intimidating drug dealers, but also sometimes were themselves the drug dealers. May 1992 saw two Brooklyn precincts in which police officers were actively selling narcotics. One of the officers involved was found to have faced allegations of corruption on at least fifteen previous occasions, yet he continued to keep his job until he was indicted.

The Mollen Commission held public hearings, then published a report. It concluded that, while a majority of police officers were honest, a small minority were corrupt, and much of the corruption involved the drug trade. The commission also found that substantiated reports of police brutality were in some ways connected with the drug traffic. For example, we found that, because of the violent nature of the drug trade, some otherwise honest police officers resorted to beating neighborhood residents to show that the police had not surrendered the neighborhood to the hoodlums. Revealing that some of these same officers slid further toward corruption and became involved in the drug traffic, a truly frightening pattern emerged. The commission's final report, published in 1994, discussed one instance in which a police officer shot a drug dealer while robbing him of his cocaine.

The Arrest of Carol Bayless

Early in the morning of April 21, 1995, a woman arrived in Washington Heights after an all-night drive from Detroit for what was not her first visit to the neighborhood. She was there—as it later turned out—to pick up some eighty pounds of cocaine and heroin, and she had with her a large amount of cash. Shortly after she double-parked her rented late-model Chevrolet Caprice, several men emerged from the shadows, where they had been waiting. They came toward the car. The woman opened the trunk and the men took a large bag from it and went into the apartment building in front of which the car was parked. Within a few minutes they returned and placed two duffel bags in the trunk. The car then began to pull slowly away.

Unknown to the driver, whose name was Carol Bayless, two police officers—Richard Carroll and Sergeant Walter Bentley—had watched intently from an unmarked police car. The entire operation, as they later testified, took place silently, with no one speaking— almost as a mime, which added to the sense of unease. Once the car pulled away, the police officers followed it closely. It turned the corner, went around the block, and returned past the house where it had stopped moments earlier. The officers slowed down and saw the men who had loaded the car. When their eyes met, the men moved away in several directions. Later testimony was conflicting as to whether the men ran or walked or simply went about their business.

Although the police car was unmarked and the officers were in plain clothes, to the men in the street it was clear who they were, and the men wanted nothing to do with them. The officers concluded that they would have little or no chance of catching the men in the darkness in their own familiar surroundings, so instead they followed the car and stopped it before it could reach the George Washington Bridge.

The officers found Carol Bayless at the wheel and asked for the usual identification. She showed them a rental-car agreement, but the contract did not identify her as the authorized driver. On that basis, they arrested Bayless and began a search of her car. In the trunk, they found 34 kilos of cocaine and 2 kilos of heroin (a kilogram or kilo equals 2.2 pounds). At that time, the street value of the drugs was more than $5,000,000.

Taken to the precinct, Bayliss made a lengthy videotaped confession. She told of her journey to New York and her intention to transport the drugs. Later, her counsel, who had not been with her at her videotaped confession, brought a motion to suppress the drugs—the only evidence the police had. He challenged whether the police had sufficient reason or suspicion for the traffic stop in the first place.

The Probable Cause Issue

Ever since the Fourth Amendment, which provides that "no warrants shall issue but upon probable cause," was ratified in 1791, probable cause has been the linchpin for immeasurable arrests. If it is found, the arrest is valid; if it is lacking, the arrest is null and void. Probable cause requires the police, before they make an arrest, to show a basis for suspecting criminal activity. If the police make an arrest and the defendant moves to suppress the evidence seized and a judge finds that at the time of the arrest the police lacked probable cause, the evidence seized during or after the arrest will be suppressed. Under what has become known as "the exclusionary rule," the prosecution at any future trial will not be allowed to introduce it. Even confessions, if there are any, are suppressed as the "fruit of the poisonous tree." While today there is an amalgam of Supreme Court pronouncements and the exclusionary rule has been watered down, if there were no such rule at all the police could fabricate charges and arrest virtually anyone, thus providing an opportunity to fish for criminal activity. Such an atmosphere would undermine our right to personal privacy.

Throughout the nineteenth and the early twentieth centuries, the court strictly construed the concept of probable cause and warned of the dangers implicit in any relaxation of that requirement. In *Olmstead v. The United States*, Chief Justice William Howard Taft suggested that to allow the police to search and seize without probable cause would be to "place the liberty of every man in the hands of every petty officer." So for many years the probable-cause requirement dominated criminal procedure and was seen as the best compromise between effective law enforcement and the interest of right to privacy.

Then, after centuries of equilibrium, the balance between privacy and effective law enforcement began to shift toward the police. The Supreme Court in *Terry v. Ohio*, with Chief Justice Earl Warren writing for the majority, created a new concept that had two conclusions: 1. that, in some circumstances, reasonable suspicion of criminal activity was sufficient to justify a stop, and 2. that the requirement of probable cause to initiate a stop was no longer the law of the land. The decision required that, for a valid stop and in order to meet the reasonable-suspicion test, the arresting officers provide "specific articuable facts."

Today even the specific articuable-fact requirement has been diluted, and many courts accept vague categories of suspicion as sufficient. For instance, reference to high-crime neighborhoods, time of day of the stop, physical mannerisms of the suspect, and sometimes even race are enough to satisfy the reasonable-suspicion test. Defendants may and do challenge the basis for a stop. Seeking the protection of the exclusionary rule, they have to meet a much higher bar than they did before *Terry*. Since then, U.S. Supreme Court decisions have taken steps to create some additional hurdles, under certain circumstances, for the police.

Was There Reasonable Suspicion?

When Carol Bayless made her fist appearance before me, she argued that the police failed the reasonable-suspicion test and that the drugs and other items seized by the police must be suppressed.

At the hearing, the government produced a single witness: Police Officer Carroll. Since the facts posed a close case and the more experienced sergeant, who acted as the reporter in the unmarked car, was never called by the government, this troubled me from the get-go. There was no corroboration of anything the young officer said. He testified to six uncorroborated facts that the government believed would be sufficient to meet the reasonable-suspicion test. They included: The car had out-of-state license plates, the neighborhood was known for drug activity, the car moved slowly and double-parked, four males crossed the street in a single line, the men put duffel bags in the trunk of the car, and they dispersed when they noticed the police officers. In addition, the government played the video confession that Bayless made at the precinct. My role in the suppression hearing was to decide whether, *at the time of the stop*, and not with the benefit of hindsight after the drugs were discovered, it was reasonable for the officers to suspect that Bayless was engaged in criminal activity.

As already mentioned, the reasonable-suspicion test is applied at the time of the stop. If this were not the case, the police would invariably pass the test because they would know with hindsight that the person arrested had in fact been engaged in criminal activity. In *Bayless*, in addition to a lack of corroboration, the testimony was riddled with inconsistencies. On that score, four points excerpted from my decision may be helpful. (Keep in mind that, although it was clearly hearsay and not subject to an exception that would have made it admissible at this juncture, the *Bayless* video was introduced by the government without objection from the defense.)

The first point is that Officer Carroll testified that he observed the defendant driving eastbound on West 176th Street. The defendant, however, maintained that she did not drive to New York City from Detroit and that she did not begin to drive the Red Caprice until after the narcotics were placed in the trunk.

Second, according to the defendant's videotaped statement, she waited ten minutes double-parked outside an apartment building on West 176th Street while the dealers took money out of the trunk, went inside to complete the transaction, and returned to put the duffle bags containing narcotics into the trunk. Officer Carroll testified that he observed the defendant as she drove along and double-parked on the north side of the street. Noticeably absent from his testimony was the ten-minute period after the car stopped and during which the men took the money from the trunk into the building and returned with the narcotics.

Third, Officer Carroll testified that he observed at least one of the males running from the scene. In marked contrast, the defendant said in her videotaped statement that, as she drove to the corner of 176th Street and St. Nicholas Avenue, she saw the males walk, not run, in the same direction.

Fourth, Officer Carroll testified that he did not observe any conversation or contact between the defendant and the males at or about the time the bags of narcotics were placed in the trunk. The defendant stated that after the males put the duffle bags in the trunk they handed her back the keys to the car so she could begin her trip home.

While it is not surprising that a defendant's recollection of the events preceding her arrest would differ from that of the arresting officer, my concern was that Bayless's statement, unlike the police version, was completely incriminating and was given immediately after the events had taken place. She had already confessed. None of the inconsistencies between her account and Officer Carroll's exonerated her in any way. She had nothing to gain by lying about what she did before the crime, or how long she waited in the car. She was not denying that she had committed a crime. Further, not only did she have no incentive to lie, but she had no opportunity to lie. When she made her statement at the police station, she had no idea what facts the police would later state as justification for reasonable suspicion. Doubtless she knew little or nothing about standards of reasonable suspicion. As to each of the discrepancies, the police officers were the only ones with something to gain; if by altering small facts they could make Bayless's activity look more unusual—more suspicious—they might pass the test and avoid suppressing the evidence.

Without any supporting evidence for a single officer's uncorroborated testimony, the government's case was based solely on Officer Carroll's story, which conflicted with the sworn confession of the defendant—who had no incentive to fabricate her story. I concluded that the officers had lacked reasonable suspicion to stop Carol Bayless's car, and therefore had made an illegal stop, so I suppressed the narcotics and the confession.

The Need for Thoughtfulness

The reaction to my decision, while it took a moment to build, can be described only as cataclysmic. This reaction was frightening to me and, more importantly, to the rule of law.

In the opinion, I set out reasons for granting the motion to suppress—e.g., the government had not provided enough evidence to support a finding that the police had reasonable suspicion to stop Carol Bayless, and the factual inconsistencies between Officer Carroll's testimony and Carol Bayless's testimony created serious questions as to the officers' justification for stopping her car. Also, the government had not provided any evidence to support Officer Carroll's testimony that the area surrounding 176th Street and St. Nicholas Avenue was a known hub to the drug trade.

Led by editorial writers across the country who had little or no knowledge of the law (and, worse yet, of the responsibility of the judge to consider the facts—regardless of how they come out—and decide cases accordingly), the print, radio, and television media attacked my decision. The fact that it was an election year may have played a role in the unrelenting—sometimes unbelievable—criticism of my decision; for example, at one point men in maroon berets picketed my home.

In a democracy, criticism of a judge's opinion is fair game, but the feeding frenzy in this instance went much further and the press was not alone. Angry citizens began sending me hate mail. They showed how the public's capacity for angst eclipsed their knowledge of the law. One woman wrote that I should be "kicked off the bench immediately for letting that woman go free with four million dollars in drugs." Of course, regardless of the outcome of the suppression hearing, the drugs are never released to the perpetrator. Another suggested I be "thrown into prison with my druggie friends." Yet another wrote that my decision gave a "clear message to criminals that their technical rights are more important in a court of law than punishment for their criminal activities." I remember one note in particular from a woman who wrote, "Yes, I know all about the constitutional rights of the perpetrators and the good intentions of our founding fathers, but that was the eighteenth century. Surely they had no idea that the twentieth century would have the kind of crime and wanton disregard for the law that we have."

This letter and many others like it, along with most of the editorials from around the country, suggested that many considered the Fourth Amendment's protections a relic of the past that had no place in the world today. I could not help but think our citizens were in large part ready to trade their liberty for security and to condemn those who were intent on saving them from themselves. While other mail and telephone calls from around the country praised the decision, the hate mail, with its apparent lack of understanding of the rule of law's central place in the fabric of our democratic way of life, was the most troubling.

I never comment on pending cases. In fact, I rarely comment after cases have concluded. In this matter, because of the publicity it generated, I did say at one point:

> The *Bayless* case was merely one of the 300 cases on my docket at the time. Sure, a large quantity of drugs was involved. But I had presided over many cases during my time as a Supreme Court Justice where large amounts of narcotics were at issue. My role in the Bayless case was the same as it was in every case that I had decided since becoming a New York State Supreme Court Justice in 1982: to make a decision based on controlling precedent, based on the facts as presented, and to resist any temptation to allow the ends to justify the means.

While the media remained focused on criticism, some Americans felt differently and spoke out. Unfortunately, except for one or two instances, their views never saw the light of day, but at least for me they were encouraging. I remember receiving the following plea:

> Please don't resign.
> We need judges who will stand up for individual liberty. We need judges who have courage. Resigning would establish a terrible precedent that federal judges serve at the whim of whichever way the political winds are blowing. This would place the judiciary on the laughable par of court systems in countries governed by dictatorships and make the Constitution meaningless.

Also among the hundreds of letters was a small package from a class of eighth graders in Elmsford, New York. The class was studying the Fourth Amendment. Recognizing the fact that crucial, often highly damaging evidence gets thrown out because of incorrect

police procedures, many students saw the central difficulty of en-
forcing the penalty—i.e., exclusion of the evidence—for a violation
of the Fourth Amendment. These young minds, no different from
many adults learning about suppression of evidence, were deeply
troubled. Samples from each side of the aisle bear repetition:

> The police clearly violated Mrs. Bayless' rights, and your deci-
> sion was justified. But on the other hand, Mrs. Bayless was
> carrying 80 pounds of drugs. She confessed to transporting
> goods several times before. You cannot let a woman who has
> committed such a severe crime just walk away. If she receives
> no punishment for her crime, she might think it's okay to do
> it again.
>
> The cop had no right at all to pull Mrs. Bayless over and
> search the trunk. His reason for searching her car trunk was
> unreasonable and at the same time he was violating the 4th
> Amendment. Yes, it is true that Mrs. Bayless had 80 pounds
> of cocaine and heroin in her trunk and yes she did admit to
> it on videotape, but all of this had to be dropped as evidence
> because the cop simply violated the rules so therefore no evi-
> dence was used.

I was amazed that eighth-grade students reading the same opinion that had sparked mass public outcry were capable of compre-
hending the basis for suppression while so many adults, seized by
fear, could not.

The Constitutional Crisis

Predictably, in an election year it was only a matter of time before politicians began to weigh in on my ruling. The Speaker of the
U.S. House of Representatives, Newt Gingrich—hardly a paragon

of constitutional law—released a statement saying, "This is the kind of pro–drug dealer, pro-crime, and anti-police and anti–law enforcement attitude that makes it so hard for us to win the war on drugs. . . . It is an astounding case." Senator Orrin Hatch was not far behind and, as a Republican and Chairman of the Senate Judiciary Committee, seized the opportunity to criticize President Bill Clinton, who had appointed me to the federal bench. "The president talks about putting cops on the beat, yet he appoints judges who are putting criminals back on the street," Hatch fumed. Senator Daniel Patrick Moynihan, who had recommended me for the federal bench, publicly stated that he regretted doing so. All this was because I dared follow the law rather than allow myself to be guided by hindsight.

Soon after my decision, the government moved for a rehearing. While a decision on that motion was pending, the frenzy picked up momentum, and on March 20, 1996, more than two hundred members of Congress, led by Representatives Fred Upton, Michael Forbes, and Bill McCollum, wrote to President Clinton requesting that he "join [them] in calling for [my] resignation from the federal bench." The letter went on to claim that my decision to suppress the narcotics and the videotaped statement—despite the quantity of drugs found, the neighborhood's bad reputation, and the police officer's observation of the men loading the trunk and fleeing— established that I had "demonstrated a level of ideological blindness that rendered me unfit for the proper discharge of my judicial duties." The scary part was the apparent panic that flowed through the halls of Congress and even the White House, and did so without mention of my legal reasoning, the factual inconsistencies in the government's case, or the lack of corroborating evidence— instead focusing only on the end result, which, they contended, could not be tolerated. The letter closed with three final points: an accusation that I had failed to "maintain [an] unbiased commitment to the rule of law," a request for the president to call for my resignation, and a pledge of legislative support for such an action—whatever that meant.

To say I was deeply troubled by the letter from Congress, which showed the utter failure of the legislators to understand the concept of the rule of law and the independent judiciary, is to put it mildly. I found it incredible that a former constitutional law professor wearing the hat of president of the United States bought it. White House spokesperson Michael McCurry publicly called the decision "wrongheaded" and pointedly said the White House was closely watching the rehearing. McCurry refused to rule out a course of action dictated by the congressional petitions, i.e., to urge my resignation. Put another way, the White House was seriously considering taking a step that was blatantly unconstitutional and unprecedented in the 220–year history of the United States.

For leading members of the judiciary, this was the last straw. Much of what judges do involves judgment. Although legislators write the law, its application to diverse real-life circumstances requires interpretation, and the analysis of evidence and testimony requires judgment. The fact that judges each have different perspectives based on different life experiences that could affect their decisions is part of what has made our judicial system envied around the world.

At the heart of judicial independence is the fact that appellate judges are responsible for scrutinizing the legal reasoning in judicial opinions. Under the U.S. Constitution, they are the appointed guardians of the rule of law. Moreover, the availability of appellate courts ensures that a person's fate never lies in only one judge's hands, and multiple levels of oversight mean that faulty decisions can be challenged and overturned.

There will always be people who disagree with any decision, and judges are tireless champions of the right to criticize decisions.

What appellate judges could not tolerate, however, was the outcry of political figures, particularly in the executive branch, seeking my resignation because of the *Bayless* ruling. That was nothing short of a direct assault on American judicial independence. For the president to suggest that the executive branch had any power to remove a judge because of a disagreement with a legal determination made in a single opinion was a startling, inconceivable breach of constitutional principles, for the U.S. Constitution guarantees life tenure to federal judges. They can be removed only through impeachment for serious crimes in breach of the public trust.

Support from Other Judges

Alarmed by the president's constitutional overstepping and exasperated by the failure of anyone else to pay attention to it, other judges and jurists began coming forward to defend me. The president of the American Association for the International Commission of Jurists, William J. Butler, wrote a letter to President Clinton, Senator Orrin Hatch, and Representative Newt Gingrich, three of my most unapologetic critics. It read, in part:

> In a democratic society, judicial decisions are not above criticism. Any judicial decision should be subject to public discussion and cannot be immune from heated commentary.
>
> However, when responsible leaders of the administration and the Congress threaten a sitting Judge with reprisal in the event that he does not reconsider a ruling in a pending case, an unwarranted intrusion into the judicial process occurs.
>
> Judicial decisions which are considered erroneous are properly dealt with through the appellate process; if tainted by corruption, bribery, or conflict of interest, impeachment proceedings provide the appropriate remedy. However, extra-

judicial attacks by elected officials which adversely affect the independence of the Judiciary are neither appropriate nor constructive.

The chief judge of the Second Circuit Federal Court of Appeals, John O. Newman, and all the living former second circuit chief judges released a powerful statement to the news media nationwide. Because it was issued by the very individuals who oversaw judicial decisions coming from my district, the statement was especially poignant. It read:

> The recent attacks on a trial judge of our Circuit have gone too far. They threaten to weaken the constitutional structure of this nation, which has well served our citizens for more than 200 years.
>
> Last Friday, the White House press secretary announced that the President would await the judge's decision on a pending motion to reconsider a prior ruling before deciding whether to call for the judge's resignation. The plain implication is that the judge should resign if his decision is contrary to the President's preference. That attack is an extraordinary intimidation.
>
> Last Saturday, the Senate Majority Leader escalated the attack by stating that if the judge does not resign, he should be impeached. The Constitution limits impeachment to those who have committed "high crimes and misdemeanors." A ruling in a contested case cannot remotely be considered a ground for impeachment.
>
> These attacks do a grave disservice to the principle of an independent judiciary, and, more significantly, mislead the public as to the role of judges in a constitutional democracy.
>
> The Framers of our Constitution gave federal judges life tenure, after nomination by the President and confirmation by the Senate. They did not provide for resignation or

impeachment whenever a judge makes a decision with which elected officials disagree.

Judges are called upon to make hundreds of decisions each year. These decisions are made after considerations of opposing contentions, arguments on both sides are often based on reasonable interpretations of the laws of the United States and the Constitution. Most rulings are subject to appeal, as is the one that has occasioned these attacks.

When a judge is threatened with a call for resignation or impeachment because of disagreement with a ruling, the entire process of orderly resolution of legal dispute is undermined.

We have no quarrel with criticism of any decision rendered by any judge. Informed comment and disagreement from lawyers, academics, and public officials have been hallmarks of the American legal tradition.

But there is an important line between legitimate criticism of a decision and illegitimate attack upon a judge. Criticism of a decision can illuminate issues and sometimes point the way toward better decisions. Attacks on a judge risk inhibiting all judges as they conscientiously endeavor to discharge their constitutional responsibilities.

In most circumstances, we would be constrained from making this statement by the Code of Conduct for United States Judges, which precludes public comment about a pending case. However, the Code also places on judges an affirmative duty to uphold the integrity and independence of the judiciary. In this instance, we believe our duty under this latter provision overrides whatever indirect comment on a pending case might be inferred from this statement (and we intend none).

We urge reconsideration of this rhetoric. We do so not because we doubt the courage of federal judges of this Circuit, or of this Nation. They have endured attacks both verbal and physical, and they have established a tradition of judicial independence and faithful regard for the Constitution that is the envy of the world. We are confident they will remain steadfast to that tradition.

Rather, we urge that attacks on a judge of our Circuit cease because of the disservice they do to the Constitution and the danger they create of seriously misleading the American public as to the proper functioning of the federal judiciary.

Each of us has important responsibilities in a constitutional democracy. All of the judges of this Circuit will continue to discharge theirs. We implore the leaders of the Executive and Legislative Branches to abide by theirs.

Suppose that things had been different. What if Judge Newman had not acted as he did? Inaction that seemed perfectly plausible under the circumstances would have accentuated the tenuous nature of our system of government—a system that needs constant attention in order to survive and prosper.

After the letter from the second circuit judges was published and aired throughout the nation, President Clinton changed course. He tried to distance himself from his earlier statement. His counsel, Jack Quinn, wrote a letter to Congressman McCollum that read:

The President believes [Baer] to be mistaken in his ruling but also believes that an independent judiciary is vitally important to the nation.

The proper way for the Executive Branch to contest judicial decisions with which it disagrees is a challenge in the courts. . . . Although comments in recent press reports may have led some to conclude otherwise, the President believes strongly that the issues before Judge Baer should be resolved in the courts.

On February 6, 1996, shortly after the president's turnaround, the government moved for a rehearing. Because I believed and had written that suppression had been granted partly due to a failure of any corroboration and I knew there might be constructive evidence in the testimony of the sergeant, I granted the motion.

Different Evidence, More Difficult Decision

A rehearing such as the one sought by the government is exceptional. Why? The theory is that both sides had their chance and, if they lost, so be it. Even when a rehearing is granted, the results rarely come out differently. It would certainly be easier to take the course of least resistance and do nothing—my champions would cheer and believe I had struck a blow for justice both social and legal. And reversing myself would provide a field day for detractors, who would immediately presume I was a wishy-washy judge who had caved in to political pressure. But I granted the application.

This time the evidence was different, which made my decision more difficult. Taking no chances, the government presented testimony from Sergeant Bentley, the more experienced of the two officers in the unmarked police car. Bentley had not testified at the original suppression hearing and had by this time read his partner's transcript. Under oath, he offered his police report into evidence, for he had been the "reporter" entrusted with the responsibility for observing and recording what transpired. In addition, the prosecution supplemented their contention that the area was a known drug-trafficking neighborhood. While they had made that assertion at the first hearing, they had done so with little or no factual support. Now they provided the court with more information.

Although Sergeant Bentley's testimony was a carbon copy of Police Officer Carroll's, it could not be disregarded—especially since it was corroborated by his police report. Further, and for reasons

I have yet to fathom, Bayless took the stand. Her testimony was inconsistent. Consequently, her credibility suffered even though it had been helpful to her in my first decision. My decision spelled out a few of what I considered the most telling examples.

> For example, in Court, Ms. Bayless testified that while she sat outside of the apartment building and the men were inside purchasing the narcotics, she saw Officer Carroll drive by her at least three times and that on the second time around she waved at the officer. Yet, in her videotaped confession, Ms. Bayless did not mention seeing Officer Carroll until after he pulled her over and approached her. Additionally, Ms. Bayless testified that while she was waiting, she had a cellular phone with her as did the men inside the building but that she chose not to use it. The Court finds it unbelievable that if the police continued to pass her car that she would have failed to call the men inside to warn them or suggest that they not bring the narcotics down to the car.
>
> As a second example, Ms. Bayless testified that while she waited for the traffic light to change from red to green at the corner of 176th Street and St. Nicholas Avenue, with Officer Carroll and Sergeant Bentley in the car behind her, a yellow cab drove up behind both vehicles and began to honk its horn once the light changed color. In marked contrast, Ms. Bayless's videotaped confession contains no mention of a yellow cab.
>
> As a third example, Ms. Bayless stated on videotape that she was not promised anything in exchange for her statement, but while on the stand, Ms. Bayless claimed that she was told that she could go home if she cooperated with the officers who questioned her. Another example of how her credibility was impaired is her testimony before this Court that the officers who questioned her at the time of her arrest repeatedly stopped the videotape if she did not provide them with

a satisfactory answer. However, a video technician performed tests on the videotape which indicate that the videotape was not stopped after the interview began and before it was concluded.

With this additional testimony and evidence from both sides, Bayless had been impeached and the government had provided corroboration for its version of the facts.

Weighing all the evidence, I did in fact reverse. This caused another media circus. The evidence at the second hearing mandated that I deny the defense motion to suppress the drugs and the confession, and that's what I did. Sadly, but not surprisingly, the media for the most part failed to realize this or read the transcript—or perhaps they didn't care. To report that I bowed to political pressure made a better story.

In the days that followed, there was of course some personal trauma to me and to my wife, including the scars left by the thoughtless editorials, but I was comfortable that the rule of law had prevailed. I was heartened by those who understood what had transpired. On that topic, Judge Newman wrote a follow-up piece in *Judicature* that read in part: "A judge concerned about public criticism might well have maintained his original ruling just to avoid condemnation by those unaware of the additional evidence presented at the hearing."

My final role in this saga came when counsel for Bayless proposed a motion for me to recuse myself. It brought yet another challenge to me and to the judicial branch of government, for it contended that the publicity precluded my objectivity—that the criticism and calls for impeachment would make it impossible for me to be fair. Again, the easy way would have been to succumb and, in a brief opinion, grant the motion. That would finish the matter and, as the saying goes, the fishmonger would the next day be wrapping fish in the newspapers that excoriated me. It would be back to business as usual. I chose not to recuse myself and concluded:

> . . . that the proper and intellectually honest approach was to continue, feeling that recusal would have certainly been easier for the court. Even where outside influence was never a part of my thinking, which is indeed the fact here, in my view not recusing myself was the far more appropriate path for a federal judge to follow.
>
> First, to be swayed by outside influence would run counter to the central theme of judicial independence. You or your client may not understand—and you are not alone—this position of the United States District Court Judge comes with life tenure. And no one, not even the President of the United States, can take it away, unless, as one great Southern District Court Judge—I think Tom Murphy—said, "They find your hand in the cookie jar."

On appeal, the Second Circuit noted that if I had disqualified myself, it could have been perceived as "a capitulation to political pressure—a capitulation, moreover, that might well have encouraged such pressure on judges in the future." The circuit also explained:

> To interpret recusal laws to mandate recusal in cases where a judge has been criticized by politicians for a controversial ruling would, in effect, confer on legislators the power to remove judges from particular cases simply by criticizing them violently. Such a reading of the statute would create a moral hazard by encouraging litigants or other interested parties to maneuver to obtain a judge's disqualification.

The circuit affirmed my decision on this motion and in each motion that I decided in *U.S. v. Bayless*.

Troublesome Information Language

I can't conclude this chapter without at least touching on the one paragraph of dicta in my opinion that raised more eyebrows and, indeed, more criticism than any other:

> Even before this prosecution and the public hearing and final report of the Mollen Commission, residents in this neighborhood tended to regard police officers as corrupt, abusive, and violent. After the attendant publicity surrounding the above events, had the men not run when the cops began to stare at them it would have been unusual.

Clearly this language was troublesome, both in terms of whether it was necessary for the opinion and whether judges, regardless of the circumstances, are required to avoid information language. Both are legitimate inquiries, and the jury is still out on the answers. Some say that this language is what makes for the much-beleaguered "activist judge." Frankly, in my experience that term is used by critics for a decision with which they disagree, and on such occasions it is equally applicable to liberals and conservatives. In this case, the concept of racial profiling jumped out at me with respect to the defendant and to the men who either walked or ran when they saw the police, who, in New York City, perform a vital function, for without them the city would likely be a lawless jungle.

Keep in mind that this incident occurred in 1995 and, unfortunately, while it bubbled somewhere near the surface, nobody dared to bring the concept and its breadth out into the light. Even after the

Obama-Gates-Crowley incident in Cambridge, Massachusetts, in July 2009—in which white police sergeant James Crowley arrested black Harvard professor Henry Louis Gates, Jr., for disorderly conduct when the professor was trying to enter his own home following a trip to China, President Obama commented on national TV that the police "acted stupidly," and then all three met for a friendly beer on the patio of the White House's Rose Garden—the concept finds little function in many communities. My decision touched on the problem and brought a wave of protest. The public is reticent about the size of the problem, yet statistics reveal that the number of black stops by the police is clearly disproportionate compared to the number of white stops.

Glenn C. Loury, a Brown University professor of economics and social science, wrote an op-ed piece that appeared in *The New York Times* on July 26, 2009. He acknowledged the difficult and vital task the police play in our society. He wrote, in a view that was mine in 1995 but that he said better some fifteen years later: "The police are our agents, charged with the imperative to control the unruly behavior of people who don't act within the norms of society. This does not excuse 'racial profiling' by police officers. It is merely to acknowledge an essential aspect of the circumstances that fuel suspicion and antipathy between black men and the police."

Professor Loury's twenty-first century concept was equally valid in the late twentieth century. Perhaps even more cogent, since I am part of our justice system, is the language of U.S. Attorney General Eric Holder. "Though this nation has proudly thought of itself as an ethnic melting pot," Mr. Holder said in a speech in 2009, "in things racial we have always been and I believe continue to be, in too many ways, essentially a nation of cowards."

My experience with *Bayless* taught me that even the best system is vulnerable and that, in order for the rule of law to function properly, we all must have faith in the process of justice and be aware that it requires constant vigilance—vigilance not just by judges and elected officials but by the public.

Much of the outcry following Bayless showed the public's and perhaps even our media's fundamental lack of faith in our justice system. They did not review the transcripts or my decision before they commented. Certainly they provided no assurance that the courts would come to the proper resolution—the just resolution. Rather, they started looking to other branches of government to intervene.

Throughout this volume, we have seen in other countries a lack of faith in the justice system, but in many of those countries there are countless concrete reasons not to trust the legal system. For example, in China the Communist Party controls the judges and actively manipulates them and their decisions for political means. In Nazi Germany, the courts were packed with loyalists who provided rulings to suit their superiors.

What common element do all these legal systems share that justifies a lack of faith? They lack judicial independence. In each system, outside influences are allowed into the courts, and judges are not free to adhere to the rule of law. Without a stable rule of law, unjust and inconsistent rulings come out of the courts, leading people to have even less faith in the legal system.

Despite *U.S. v. Bayless*, I am optimistic about the future of the American judiciary. There will be many other obstacles threatening our system and the systems of other countries, but, given the safeguards provided by our Constitution, so long as we truly and completely believe in and support the system, judicial independence can and will prevail.

8

The Face of an Independent Judiciary

TAKE A LOOK AT THESE NAMES AND THINK WHAT QUALITIES COME
to mind: Louis D. Brandeis, Benjamin N. Cardozo, Learned Hand,
John Marshall Harlan, Oliver Wendell Holmes, John Marshall, and
Thurgood Marshall. Some of these judges are known for scholar-
ship, some for writing skill, some for standing up for principle.
Each is respected for independence.

What makes a judge independent? A combination of personality and job security. The personality comes in large measure from a
combination of influences: parents, teachers, inspiring role models,
and a good grasp of human history. Job security insulates and pro-
tects judges from outside pressures—from officials, politicians, the
news media.

Alexander Hamilton understood this, and he gave us probably
our greatest constitutional principle: Section 1 of Article III, adopted in 1789 (note that punctuation and capitalization of key
words are from the original).

Article III
    Section 1. The judicial Power of the United States, shall
be vested in one Supreme Court, and in such inferior courts
as the Congress may from time to time ordain and establish.

The Judges, both of the supreme and inferior Courts, shall hold their Offices during good Behaviour, and shall, at stated Times, receive for their Services, a Compensation, which shall not be diminished during their Continuance in Office.

Federal judges have varying skills and character traits, but they are all the same in one important respect: They are appointed for life and their salaries cannot be reduced. They have absolute job security and are free to exercise independent judgment. This is an essential part of public trust and confidence in our system of justice.

Let me spell out some specifics. While obviously these notions can't assure independence, they may make a difference. They may make it a little more likely that judges will act independently. Clearly, where provided with the proper tools, it will be easier to embrace the concept. These ideas, while not new to us in the federal judiciary, must be part of any effort by nations struggling to provide for their own independent judiciary.

1. Selection process
   Acceptable options
   a. Appointment by executive, subject to confirmation by the legislature, following public hearings
   b. Popular election under a multiple-party system
   c. Merit selection (i.e., appointment by executive from limited list of candidates pre-screened by independent committee).

2. Job security
   Necessary elements
   a. Lengthy term of years, or life tenure ("during good behavior")
   b. Salary fixed at an upper-middle income level, not to be

diminished and with the assurance of annual additions to offset increases in cost of living, plus health care and retirement benefits

   c. Immunity from arrest, removal, or impeachment, except on public charges and fair trial.

3. Judicial powers
   Minimum requirements
   a. Power to issue writs of *habeas corpus*
   b. Power to enforce individual rights and freedoms.

For the reader interested in a fuller discussion of the necessary ingredients for judicial independence and availability, an excellent source is *International Principles on the Independence and Accountability of Judges, Lawyers and Prosecutors—A Practitioners' Guide* (Geneva, Switzerland: International Commission).

Providing job security for judges is only part of the process of developing an independent judiciary. A courageous and independent body of lawyers is another essential ingredient. Why is this essential? Henry L. Stimson, who served the U.S. as Secretary of State as well as Secretary of War, explained it in his memoir *On Active Service in Peace and War*:

Through many channels I came to learn and understand the noble history of the profession of the law. I came to realize that without a bar trained in the traditions of courage and loyalty our constitutional theories of individual liberty would cease to be a living reality. I learned of the experience of those many countries possessing constitutions and bills of rights similar to our own, whose citizens had nevertheless lost their liberties because they did not possess a bar with sufficient courage and independence to establish those rights by a brave assertion of the writs of habeas corpus and certiorari. So I came to feel that the American lawyer should regard himself as a potential officer of his government and a defender of its laws and constitution. I felt that if the time should ever come when this tradition had faded out and the members of the bar had become merely the servants of business, the future of our liberties would be gloomy indeed.

How Can We Help?

To establish an independent bench, the fundamental challenge is to create an independent legal profession from which independent judges can be recruited. First, however, comes independence at the bar. Without that, an independent judiciary is powerless to halt torture or any other abuse of human rights.

Judicial independence in America's own system is itself a fragile commodity. Nonetheless, its fragility ought not stop us from making an effort to help other nations become familiar with the notions we rely on to promote the rule of law. We get it right most of the time.

One possible contribution would be well-funded internships for foreign students to study how to protect legally enforced civil rights and help people gain and enjoy personal freedom (e.g., legal aid, public defenders, poverty law offices, prosecution offices, ACLU, class-action law firms). Fellowships would be geared to develop confidence in our legal system and in how to oppose misuse of police power and political authority. Foreign students who have leadership potential in their home countries could then become catalysts for change.

We cannot lose sight of low-cost worldwide communications, so available via the Internet and other wireless technologies. This vehicle offers new opportunities to create popular demand for an independent judiciary. In native languages, non-commercial public education communications can teach people the essentials of civil rights, such as:

- no unlawful search and seizure,
- no arrest and detention without a hearing,
- the right to confront one's accuser,
- the right to counsel.

Technology also provides a two-way street for getting information to the outside world about repressive practices, thereby generating pressure on governments to strengthen the protection of human rights.

The people's demand for civil rights, and for lawyers and judges to make those rights real, is the single most important goal. In his World War II–era talk in 1944 to a group of newly naturalized U.S. citizens, Judge Learned Hand said it better than anyone:

What do we mean when we say that first of all we seek liberty? I often wonder whether we do not rest our hopes too much upon constitutions, upon law and upon courts. These are false hopes, believe me, these are false hopes. Liberty lies in the hearts of men and women; when it dies there, no constitution, no law, no court can save it; no constitution, no law, no court can even do much to help it. While it lies there it needs no constitution, no law, no courts, to save it.

Acknowledgments

Although the final work of pulling this book together took only a few months, the idea had percolated over many years. The need and inspiration for it came from Whitney North Seymour, Jr., my friend and mentor for more than fifty years. In his fight for justice, he is tireless, and I was proud to serve as his First Assistant and Chief of the Criminal Division when he was the United States Attorney for the Southern District of New York. At his urging, I assembled a group of interns and former law clerks, and we met in my chambers early in the morning on several occasions to choose topics for this book, to assign research projects, and to review initial drafts of chapters. Those who made significant contributions included Dara Sheinfeld, a recent law clerk (who on occasion brought her infant daughter with her); Amanda Gilman; and Graham O'Donoghue. I gratefully acknowledge the contributions of each of these talented young collaborators, who researched and wrote first drafts and several chapters.

My role was to encourage research and eventually make some order out of all the material. In the midst of this effort, I was privileged to interview Judge Leposava Karamarkovic in Belgrade and to have a detailed conversation with Mr. Guo, a Chinese lawyer driven out of his country by the Communist government. They each added immeasurably to my understanding of what courage means—more particularly, courage where the rule of law is threatened. Whatever order resulted is due in large part to Bernard Ryan, Jr., who was tireless in his effort to edit and accommodate additions and corrections and who actually put the book into its present form. In addition, Marc Jaffe, a nationally known and revered editor, gave generously of his time.

I want to acknowledge that the book *Constitutional and Political History of Pakistan*, by Hamid Khan, was most helpful in framing the discussion in chapter 5.

Finally, after I spoke at a program at George Mason School of Law, my rather fragmented notes, along with those of the other speakers, were edited and became Volume 4, No. 1, of *The Journal of Law, Economics & Policy*, published by George Mason University. My contribution was so well done that I invited the editor in chief of the *Journal*, Dean Lhospital, to work with me on this book. I owe him a debt of gratitude for the time he donated to this effort and his way with words. He contributed historical flourish and scholarship to the manuscript.

Appendix

Interview with Mr. Thomas G. Guo,

November 21, 2005

Judge: Hello?

Guo: Hello? Judge, how are you?

Judge: I'm good. I'm glad you're finally with us. I don't know what the problem is, Mr. Guo, with your number, but it certainly doesn't seem to work.

Guo: Oh, there. I, uh, I don't know what, what is wrong with it. My phone number is a, is normal, I think.

Judge: In any event, we've got you now. And Dara, uh, my former clerk who's working with me is also on the phone, I believe.

Dara: I'm here.

Judge: O.K.

Guo: O.K.

Judge: All right, so you're kind to let us ask you some questions, and you should take as long as you want to answer them, and hopefully this will not take more than an hour. I wrote to you most of my concerns, so if you can just tell us a little bit about your life, do you get *The New York Times* in Vancouver?

Guo: Oh, I didn't go to New York until now.

Judge: Ah, there's just been a number of articles which follow along the lines of your treatment in China that have been in the *Times* recently. There was a full, almost a full-page article on the 12th of November. I'll send it to you. Anyway, tell me about yourself.

Guo: Uhhh . . .

Judge: Like, when were you born and where?

Guo: O.K. I say, I would like answer your questions according to your interview questionnaire, O.K.?

Judge: Yes.

Guo: Yes, I was born in Fujian. Fujian Province in China, of course, in 19—1958, January 10th. So, when I, when I was uh, became a law school student I, was shortly sent to the countryside for four years, where I became a worker. A truck-repair mechanic. And then I became a teacher. Middle-school teacher, a physical-ed teacher. In 1980 I, I went to, went into Jilin University. Majored in international law. Then, after four years study I became, I graduated from that university. And was sent by the government of China to the Fujian Province as a judge. But just before I went to the court, I was told my job changed. I was to be a lawyer instead of judge.

Judge: You could make that decision?

Guo: I cannot make decision.

Judge: Oh.

Guo: Because the government is control everything. I have no choice. Before this I was being sent to Fujian Province as a judge but when I went to be a judge, Fujian high court told me I have to move, you know, change my job to be a lawyer instead of judge.

Dara: But, what was the reason?

Guo: No reason at all. Because someone, someone drive me out. In China, there are, this situation is always happen. If someone have a good relationship with the high court, they can easily kick me out. Because I have, I have no relation with this high court, so this is the reason. It's very easy.

Dara: But was it because they needed more lawyers and they didn't need as many judges? Or did they know something about your background that they didn't want you to be a judge?

Guo: No, no, it's simply because during that time to be a judge is a very good job so many people compete for that very position. So someone behind me, I don't know how can he do that. He just drive me out. Drive me out. He himself want to go to the high court of Fujian Province. So I became a lawyer in 1984. This is my very brief, before I became a lawyer story. But for me, to be a jud . . . a lawyer actually is not depend on my choice, it's just a because I have a no idea what is lawyer and what is judge at the time. So actually, I am, I'm preferred to be a professor or to be a judge. I have to say honestly, until now I think I would be a very good professor or a very good judge. Not a good lawyer.

Judge: Well, but at this time, Mr. Guo, in 1984, or five, as I inquired in my titles, I wondered whether there were any prohibitions or any guarantees like in our Constitution with respect to searches and seizures and counsel.

Guo: I beg your pardon?

Judge: When you became a lawyer, were there any kinds of rights that we have here against unlawful searches and seizures, or did the government pretty much do what it chose in terms of searching and seizing. And with respect to counsel. What was the status in '85 of the right to counsel?

Guo: In 1985 I was a trainee, not a lawyer.

Judge: Well, when you became a lawyer.

Guo: Yes, I became a lawyer actually I became a qualified lawyer only two years later. I begin training in 1984 and in 1986 I passed the examination to be a lawyer then I became a qualified lawyer. Since 1984 I became a practice as a lawyer. So I'm not qualified lawyer then, but I can appear in court as a trial lawyer too during that time. So, at the very beginning I am actually as a criminal defense lawyer.

Judge: And how did that, how did you feel about that in terms of being able to protect your clients?

Guo: At that time I think that the court, the judges, were better than now.

Judge: Oh, really?

Guo: Yes, at that time. Although their education level was lower, their moral standards were higher than now. Here, now in China the legal system I think turned to, turned to not good, turned to bad, turned to worse.

Judge: Like how, how do you mean?

Guo: I mean, that actually nowadays a judge most of them, more judge graduate from the university, in 1984 many judge just come from army men. They resign from army, and receive only three months training, law training then became judge. Of course their, ability is qualified, is not a qualified judge at the time. But many, many judges are good at the time. So from in very beginning I have, I remember that during the first two or three years at least I have handled about thirty, criminal law, criminal cases. I win the cases a lot of. And win at least 70 percent I win, I win the cases at the time. Of course it's not, just because I'm very hard working lawyer of course, I prepare for my cases very carefully, and spend a lot of times and focus to my cases.

Judge: Were there juries? There are not juries.

Guo: No jury at all, of course. Only, only three judge is all, one judge, and two so-called People's Jury, in China. But actually they have no rights, they even during the whole trial the People's Jury speak nothing and only the judge to decide it.

Judge: Don't they have a vote?

Guo: Uh, they have the right to vote. But they will agree with the judge's idea, of course. So, that time, even in the very beginning, my case always win, not lose. I turn to the commercial lawyer just because for money. Because as a criminal lawyer we earn nothing. Very very limited fee of lawyer for criminal law cases, very lower at the time.

Judge: Is that provided by the state? I mean, these are poor defendants who can't afford to pay you?

Guo: No, no, no. Lawyer's fee just pay by the crimes. That time, only 30, 30, getting one criminal cases lawyers can earn only 30 ren min bi. 30 RMB. Always, of course, very limited money. But actually, at that time, lawyer's salary came from government, not from the client. The client pay the fee through the government. As a lawyer, we will receive our salary from the government at the time.

Dara: What if the defendant had no money? Could he get a lawyer?

Guo: If there, I don't know at that time what the situation is. But most of the cases they will pay, they will pay the fee because the fee is so limited, if not so expensive. It's very cheap at the time. But now, nowadays my knowledge is that many, many poor client they can receive so-called legal aid from government. Legal aid coming from government is just a court-appointed lawyer as a defense lawyer for the poor, poor criminal, kind.

Judge: And what do they receive? Do they get an hourly fee from the government?

Guo: Not hourly, government will pay the lawyer a very limited fee.

Judge: Like, how much would that be in dollars?

Guo: They are counted not upon timely, just upon one case by one case. For example, if you handle one case for robbery, you would receive about 800 RMB now in China.

Judge: And now is it very different?

Guo: Still today there are a lot of people who cannot receive legal aid especially for the sensitive case and for the political cases no legal aid at all is provided. For example, when I was dealing with some cases for political reasons, political criminal, they are very poor, and their family also very poor, they even cannot pay legal fee to the lawyer. Government also refuse to pay such fee.

Judge: So they don't get any representation at all, or their lawyer doesn't get paid at all.

Guo: Just because government has forbidden, even forbidden lawyers to defend such kinds of clients.

Judge: And how are judges selected today in China, Mr. Guo?

Guo: Oh, I would like to say something about the selection of judge in China is quite a different from the theory and practice. It's a different thing. From the theory and the law, the selection of judges is supposed to be according to qualifications, their law education, and their moral standard and ability but actually, many judge just come from the, as mentioned, from the army men. And a lot of the judges were clerks, they are working in the, working in the, in the court for several years and later they become judge.

Judge: A-ha.

Guo: Even in Superior Court, I observed that there is a woman judge that formally she is a clerk, she was a secretary of the Superior Court. Now she became a Superior Court judge.

Judge: Did she go to law school before that?

Guo: No, no, no, no law school at all.

Judge: Uh huh.

Guo: And so it's a very strange right? In 1995, there is a law passed, a judge law that is a, which decides, which stipulate how to select a judge. So now, to my knowledge that this judge is just a send from the university, graduate from university, they go to the court directly into the district court, then the high court, and the Superior Court. It means that out of the same class the student will be sent to different level court to be a judge. So it's not a good way. It's unfair. So many good judge, and excellent judge have no, no hope to promotion because they, the position was occupied by the other many unqualified lawyers on a judge.

Judge: How long do they stay as judges?

Guo: Mm hm?

Judge: Once they, once they are appointed, how long is their term?

Guo: Oh, this term in theory is a long term. It will be for life. But actually it's not. For example, the, the judge, in the Judge Law, Article 8 of Judge Law says they stipulate that without the reason of law, law stated clearly, and without the law, um, no, without through the procedure, the law procedure, the judges are not untenuous or lower degree or force resign or punishment. But actually, under the same law Article 14, the Judge Law Article 14 states that the judge could be fired, or force resign for following reason: one is that annual test constituted the two years not qualify as a judge, or not fit for the current work, or while and [*unintelligible*] accepted the other arrangement for trial agency of [*unintelligible* adjustment?*] [*unintelligible* for rav just need of adjustment?*]. I refuse to reasonable rearrangement out of the work for constituting fifteen days or account for thirty days a year will be refused as uh, I'll be refused to perform the duties of the judge and after the education, still without any improvement. In both this reason, the judge will lose their job, or will be changed or will be fired. So the judge are supposed to be life tenured, it is only a theory. Actually, how can say that judge will clear to part any examination, any test, if someone is not qualified as a judge how can he become a judge? This is ridiculous, of course I think.

Judge: What about the role of the Communist Party? Do they have any role in who becomes a judge?

Guo: Oh, you mention it a key point. In China the legal system or the judge, the court, the most serious problem is that the communist party control everything. Communist Party control in China's court system, and actually, to my knowledge almost 100 percent of judge have to be communist party members. This is the reason why in China they have no rule of law, and no rule of justice, no judicial justice at all. Especially for the sensitive cases, or the criminal cases, e.g., the Falun Gong cases. All are under control of the CCP, under [*unintelligible* trial?] to the judge, but to no justice will be, will be [*unintelligible* construed?]. Because the CCP, um, the communist party control everything. For example, I would like to show a very, very example. One of my clients he's a young man who organized a party on the Internet—O.K., I want to say, so uh this case go into the court have a hearing. All the judge, three judge are Communist Party members. But my client is, he organized a party against the Communist Party. So we are apply for change of judge. We asked for non-party member judge to try this case but it was refused by the court. Of course we lose the case. Someone who is against the Communist Party being tried by a CCP member, how can, how can, we expect any justice? Of course, of course not.

Judge: Well, when you say that, Mr. Guo, was that a case in which you think some of your problems arose, or as a consequence of that case that your problems with the government began to occur?

Guo: Yes. Yes. I just mentioned this case as one of the reason the government of China punish me. They say I openly, openly claimed for it to end the one party dictatorship system. And they uh, curse me, how they asked do you dare to ask for non-party member judge to try this case? This is the, this is the reason, one reason they punish me. That's why. Of course, I persist in my idea, my opinion, judge should be non-party member. Judge should not listen to anyone else, just listen to the law, not listen to any party's idea. Only in this way, there is a justice.

Judge: Well, I, but I presume from what you have said that if they had ruled in your favor, they would have been either demoted or transferred. Is that true? The judges?

Guo: The judges?

Judge: If they had ruled in your favor, and said, "O.K., we're going to send you to a judge that's not a party member," then they would have been punished.

Guo: Well, but actually it is impossible for the court to choose non-party member for judge because there is no one who can become a judge if he is not a communist party member. In China.

Judge: How long ago did you begin to have problems? When was this, when was this case that you're telling us about, how many years ago?

Guo: It's a long story. I was, I was, actually I was punished by a, punished, punished by the China authority for four times. Not only once. In lots of times I was forced to leave China. The first punishment that follow me was in 1987. In 1987 only for a letter, a letter, I sent to my girlfriend. My girlfriend betrayed me. In this letter, I criticized the community party, so-called democratic, democracy, and so-called dictatorship. My girlfriend, maybe she is a party member, so she betray me and handed this letter to the, to the, justice bureau. Then I lose my, no, the authority suspended my lawyer's license for one year that time. This happened in my lawyer's career in 1987.

Judge: Who, who did that? What body can suspend your license?

Guo: It's the justice bureau of Fujian Province.

Judge: And they just write you a letter and say you're suspended or do you have a hearing?

Guo: Oh, no hearing, no hearing at all, only, only, only denounce, decision. No appear and no hearing the time, just a suspend my lawyer's license for one year.

Judge: And that was in '87?

Guo: Uh, yes, that was first time.

Judge: And then, what was the next time that you got into difficulty practicing law?

Guo: Next time, when I, one year later when I recovered my lawyer's license again, I practice again of course. Then in 1995 I made my second trouble. This time I am the attorney of a Hong Kong company, an international export and import company, and this case last for sixteen years until, up to date and it's still not ours. There's no final result even today the case went from the Xiamen middle court to the Fujian high court then finally to a superior court. As a lawyer for the Hong Kong company, I did in this case, and I win the first sentence, then [*unintelligible* failed to appear?]. Then we appeared to the superior court in Beijing. Then Beijing high . . . superior court decide that the Fujian high court judgment is wrong. So, they hold a hearing in 1998 but until now up to date they didn't give the final judgment. During this case, defendant's lawyer, who is a Beijing lawyer, but his father is the Justice Minister of China and also he's a security department, the highest security department of China, and also who the superior court vice chief judge, so he's through the Justice Minister of China punish me again. And uh, force me to recognize I'm wrong in something [*unintelligible* I left?], or I will lose my lawyer's license again. I refuse to accept their treatment this time. So they suspended my lawyer's license for half a year. Only in 1996 when I opened a law firm of my own, they had to return back to my lawyer's license. This is the second time I [*unintelligible* been into another trouble?]

Judge: And you think that was because you wouldn't reverse your position about your client's rights?

Guo: Yes, I refuse, I refuse to surrender. I refuse to give up my case.

Judge: I see.

Guo: Because I think my case is a 100 percent I have to win this case. The defendants just make, make up the evidence, they make up a lot of the evidence or [*unintelligible* not to choose?]. So this case of course is very founders in China.

Judge: And, that case is still going on? There's no final decision?

Guo: Yeah, now it's fifteen or sixteen years since start.

Judge: And that was the third time that you found yourself punished?

Guo: The third time happens in 1997. 1997 I became a defense attorney for a Hong Kong company general manager who was charged by the government of Fuzhou and faced charge of theft of 100 million U.S. dollar through the contract. But actually, when I do some investigation and I learn a great deal of the evidence, I know that this case is ordinary contract dispute. It's not a criminal case at all. But the Fuzhou security department detained my client and arrested her and arrested her sister, the other one who has none business with the case. Just to force my client to surrender, and force her to pay back dollars. So I became this company, this Hong Kong company's lawyer again and my, I am challenging the Fuzhou government, Fuzhou city, government, and Fuzhou public security, and in this case, also is quite famous in China. During that time Fuzhou security department threatened me several times and through four friends tell me that I was under black list and finally they even threaten me to take my life if I go on with this case. So, as a defense lawyer, represented my clients in the first hearing, and when we are to appear before the high court my client asked me to stop. He say security department threatened him if he engaged me to go on with the case and told him, we will punish him the client even more so I resigned. But the security department still didn't give up their threats toward me, they even make some trouble about their traffic accident, one to take me to the end of my life. So, finally, in 1999 I moved from Fujian—

Judge: This is because you were suing the government?

Guo: Yes, because I'm suing government of Fuzhou, and security department of Fuzhou.

Judge: And so you moved out?

Guo: So finally, I move out, I leave, I left Fujian Province.

Judge: But did they take your license away a third time?

Guo: No, they are not taken my license away, but they want to take my life away.

Judge: Yes, I gather.

Guo: So, in this way I give up my own law firm in Fuzhou and went to Shanghai to start my lawyer's business again.

Judge: You have to keep your voice up because I'm barely hearing you, Mr. Guo. You went to Shanghai and you opened a firm again, a new firm?

Guo: Yes, I went to Shanghai in the very, at first not open my law firm again, only three years later in 2002 I opened my own law firm again in Shanghai. In 2003 January, I decided to turn my business from maritime lawyer to human rights lawyer again, to become a human rights lawyer. So this bring me fourth big trouble again. But I like it, I like it, I prefer to be a human rights lawyer.

Judge: But you knew that that would probably get you in trouble, right?

Guo: Yes, I knew it, of course I knew it. I knew it. But to be a human rights lawyer is my job, so I like it, and I like the challenge. So, so since 2003 until generally I became a writer on Internet in Chinese lawyer's net, and I became the number one writer in, I mean, the most welcome writer in that net. In Chinese lawyer's net, a lot of young Chinese lawyers there, they always discuss and argue with me a lot of the questions about the law and political and legal system and justice. So in this way I like it very much, and I learn so many people just because they express their ideas, their opinion, about politics, about social matters. They were under arrested and detained and even put into centers and even sentenced for several years. The first one is a student, who is a student in Beijing, teachers normally in college, and she is only a third year graduate student, but she was arrested secretly and her name was Liu Ti, and is very famous in Internet.

Judge: Let me stop you there for a minute. One of the articles that I read recently talks about something called administrative detention. And essentially, it was putting a son of this man in jail without any hearing at all, and for a fairly long period of time he just was there without any charges being leveled against him. Is that something that you have had any connection with or watched or seen or heard about?

Guo: Oh, such kind of, what you say is, uh—

Judge: Administrative detention is what it's called in this article.

Guo: I have read that article, too. This type of situation in China is I think common phenomena. It's not so seldom. Actually a lot of the clients were suffer this situation because they are poor, very poor, and then they are not famous and they suffer a great deal, nobody know it. And no one concerned with it. In this way, local authority always want to do something to escape their duty, and they want to see some so-called criminal, and maybe this guy is not criminal at all, they just want to, want to, in this way if some [*unintelligible*] case happen and the police cannot detain someone then the people will be very angry with them; they will say policemen do nothing. So someone, some place, the policemen do such thing. They just seize someone and put him in jail then say they have resolved the problem. This is why. So I return back to my topic?

Judge: All right, please go ahead, tell us the rest of your story.

Guo: O.K., just because I mentioned that.

Judge: Yes.

Guo: After [*unintelligible*] several young people in Beijing and in Chang Chui, and in Hubei all together they [*unintelligible*] one Du Tao Ping. Du Tao Ping was arrested for he published essays on Internet. So I openly support him in Chinese lawyer's net, and

I offer myself to be defense lawyer for them. I also met a lawyer whose name is Bei Jing Chang in, his net name is Liu Lu, we both act as sponsors and open a, no made a petition to the HuqinTao to appear the overturn government the power, that's a criminal law, so in this way Mr. Liu lose his job. He his lawyer's license was seized by the Shangdong justice bureau in 2003.

INDEX

ABOUT THE AUTHOR

HAROLD BAER, JR., is a judge of the United States District Court. In 1992, he resigned from the New York State Supreme Court after serving on that bench for ten years. For two years before his induction as a District Court judge, he was the executive judicial officer at JAMS/Endispute (Judicial Arbitration and Mediation Services), where he supervised the staff and other mediators and arbitrators and did dispute resolution himself. For a decade before his election to the Supreme Court, he was in charge of litigation in a Wall Street law firm. In the 1960s, he was an assistant United States attorney and headed the Organized Crime and Racketeering Unit of that office; he returned in 1970 as first assistant U.S. Attorney and chief of the Criminal Division. Judge Baer served on the five-person Mollen Commission, investigating police corruption from 1992 through 1994. After Mayor John V. Lindsay formed the Civilian Complaint Review Board of the New York City Police Department, Judge Baer was its first executive director. He has been active in New York State, City, and County Bar Associations, chairing committees for each, as well as serving as a trustee of the Federal Bar Council. He was the founder of the Network of Bar Leaders and president of the New York County Lawyers Association. In addition to hundreds of published opinions, he has written extensively on legal topics, with some fifty books, pamphlets, and articles to his credit. His most recent book, coauthored with

Robert Meade and titled *Depositions—Practice and Procedure in Federal and New York State Courts*, was published in 2005 by the New York State Bar Association. He graduated, magna cum laude and Phi Beta Kappa, from Hobart College and, in 1957, from the Yale Law School.